AF334475

THE CORAL

GEORG KAISER

THE CORAL

A Play in Five Acts

Introduction by
VICTOR LANGE
Princeton University

FREDERICK UNGAR PUBLISHING CO.
NEW YORK

Published by arrangement with
Verlag Kiepenhauer & Witsch, Köln

Translated by Winifred Katzin

Copyright 1963 by
Frederick Ungar Publishing Co., Inc.

Printed in the United States of America

Library of Congress Catalog Card No. 63-12906

INTRODUCTION

THE CHANGES in feeling and perception that began to take shape among the poets and painters at the turn of this century, culminating in the revolutionary drama of German expressionism, can hardly be more effectively illustrated than by Georg Kaiser's *Gas*. Uncompromising in its break with the dramaturgical conventions of the psychological play that had reached its perfection in the achievements of Ibsen, Kaiser's work is cast in a form carefully calculated to convey a modern issue: it is concerned not with the alternatives of individual behavior but with the collective experience of a moral crisis brought about by the consequences of contemporary economic and technological practices.

It is not surprising that this theme should have been stated most bluntly by the German writers of the early twenties. A once vigorous and self-confident society found itself disintegrating in the wake of the defeat of 1918; and the subsequent turmoil of political upheaval and economic collapse created the climate for desperate outbursts of imaginative energy. Much of that expressionist literature is utopian: it devoted itself to a scrutiny of those human resources that might help in the rebuilding of what had been destroyed, and it turned fervently and even angrily to an analysis of those forces that seemed most inimical to a better life. But where it advanced beyond a bitter denunciation of the past, it proclaimed an image of the human being which, naive and unduly idealistic though it may seem, yet projected an order of society in which sentient and compassionate man was to be the master and not the victim of his own aspirations.

It is clear that so intense and radical a vision should excite, above all, the sensibilities of the lyrical poets, in whose work the double cry of accusation and hope can be heard again and again. But where the revolutionary message is proclaimed not merely with fervor and faith but as a challenge to be dialectically argued, it produced a curiously persuasive type of theatre. In the plays of some of these authors, lyricism and ideological convictions are often intermingled; others are less sentimental but aggressively critical of middle-class beliefs; only Georg Kaiser, an immensely productive and versatile playwright, succeeded in maintaining an artistic balance between the passion of the social revolutionary, an incorruptible eye for the logic inherent in an intellectual proposition, and the technical skill of an expert in theatre.

George Kaiser was born in Magdeburg, Germany, in 1878. As the son of a well-to-do merchant his business career seemed assured: he was sent to Argentina to work for one of the largest German power concerns, but, after three years in Buenos Aires, his health failing, he returned to Europe and lived in Italy and Spain before settling in the vicinity of Berlin. During the twenties he was the most productive of the German playwrights, and in 1930 was elected to the German Academy—a distinction of which the Nazi government deprived him four years later. Being in his social views sharply in conflict with the prevailing political climate in Germany, he emigrated to Switzerland. He continued to produce plays, fiction, and poetry. Much of his later work is not yet available in print; but it is clear that the work of his last fifteen years differs in many respects from those plays that established his reputation as an "expressionist" writer. He died in Ascona in 1945.

Kaiser's career is not easily summarized, nor has his total achievement yet received adequate critical treatment. In more than seventy plays—thirteen of them produced in 1917-18 alone—ranging from brittle comedies to savage attacks upon the delusions of his age, from modern farces to sustained tragedies in the Greek manner, he deals again and again with the forces of unreason and delusion that threaten contemporary man. Kaiser is first and foremost a moralist: his theme is the "renewal of man," the search for those authentic qualities in the human being that will prove durable and creative beyond the paralysis of judgment.

Like Gerhart Hauptmann, Kaiser is a social dramatist without doctrinaire convictions; but, different from Hauptmann, he limits the scope and mobility of the individual and subjects it to the inexorable logic of circumstance and technical realities. In one of his early plays, *From Morn Till Midnight* (1916), Kaiser examines, in a series of highpitched scenes, the pathetic efforts of a bank teller who breaks out of his routine existence to find meaning and integrity. No familiar form of social life can provide it for him: he can in the end assert it only for himself. He dies a martyr in a sacrificial act of self-destruction.

Gas (1917-20) is a dramatic project of greater scope and intensity. It consists of three plays, *Die Koralle*, *Gas I*, and *Gas II*.

In *The Coral* (1917), the first of the three plays, the theme of integrity—the utopian vision of the "new man"—is elaborated in the context of an individual life. Kaiser shows in a series of carefully contrived scenes the climax of a harassed life: the millionaire (or, as Kaiser with characteristic overemphasis calls him, the billionaire) has all his life been in flight from poverty and exploitation. Now he has at last achieved immense wealth and, through it, something like protection against the terrors of his childhood, terrors from which he hopes to spare his son. But the son turns against the life of power through exploitation and joins the workers.

Through a curious and effective theatrical conceit Kaiser provides the billionaire with a double who acts as his secretary—an alter ego whose happy childhood distinguishes him from his employer. In order to "adopt" his identity, the billionaire kills his secretary, and the coral fob which the secretary wore on his watch chain becomes the symbol of an authentic life. For the sake of this symbol he is willing to die as a murderer: "We are forever driven; we are exiles from our paradise of silence, pieces broken loose from the coral tree of life, wounded on the very first day." A state of mind beyond fear and anguish Kaiser seems here to argue, must remain a dream embodied in the token of the coral.

The execution of the tycoon is, of course, no resolution of the sense of futility in which, as Kaiser sees it, his furious capitalistic struggle has engulfed him; it is merely the gesture of renunciation so characteristic of many expressionist plays by which an intolerable life is canceled out and a return to a state of nirvana is achieved.

Gas I advances the argument from a private issue to a group experience: the son of the "billionaire" has become a social revolutionary, dedicated to the realization of the "new man." He offers his workers the opportunity of a humane life if they will agree to abandon the production of gas upon which the huge machinery of capitalism depends but which threatens from time to time to destroy the workers' community. At the risk of their happiness the workers prefer the "system" to "life": the new man is not yet.

For in *Gas II* (1920) the world is engulfed in apocalyptic destruction: the impact of fanatical technological thinking upon the human being is demonstrated most dramatically. The great-grandson of the billionaire is now one of the workers in a state run plant; in an effort at preventing imminent total war he proclaims the ideals of meekness and brotherly love instead of self-ambition and battle. He fails. Not victory but radical destruction of both warring sides is the inescapable result. The voice of the visionary cries in a wilderness of inhumanity: beyond the evidence of barbarism he can only project a dream of peace in another world.

The three plays, each artistically and intellectually complete in itself, may at first sight seem profoundly skeptical of the very idealism that constituted the chief impulse of the German expressionist poet. Yet they provide in fact the poetic elaboration, in extreme images and situations, of the economic and social implications of capitalism as Kaiser and the German revolutionary intelligentsia saw them after the First World War. The exploitational character of money and the concomitant paralysis of the individual leaves the billionaire in *The Coral* with only the essentially romantic desire for self-extinction; in *Gas I* his son proclaims an ethical socialism which is doomed to failure in the face of collective blindness and the compelling or persuasive interests of the state; in *Gas II* state socialism itself leads to a holocaust in which the "blue figures" of capitalism and the "yellow figures" of socialism extinguish one another. None of these forms economic and political organization seem tolerable: the billionaire-worker in *Gas II* is the "new man" who accepts the inevitable "eccentricity" of an absolute conviction of human integrity. He knows that he must continue to proclaim it as a platonic truth, an "inner realm" of meaning, to which any future must refer.

Thus the central motif of these three plays is the clash between a stubbornly maintained vision of truth and the seductive and often overwhelming compulsions of power—the power of individual satisfaction, the power of wealth, and power in its harshest and most technical modern form, exercised for its own sake.

It is true that Kaiser insists that "the deepest wisdom is found only by a single mind. And when it is found it is so overwhelming that it cannot become effective." Yet, the issue which Kaiser argues concerns all of us, it is not a private one; its moral impact cannot therefore, as in the plays of Ibsen and Hauptmann, be shown in a series of individual experiences with which we as spectators might identify ourselves. Indeed, Kaiser is not primarily concerned with the alternatives of action or judgment that might be open to a well-defined character; his purpose is altogether the unraveling of the implications of an intellectual position. Each turn of events, every sentence that is uttered, is, therefore, in Kaiser's plays, a key to an essentially dialectical intention. His plots are exactly developed elaborations of his central ideas. This is to say that the dramatic structure of the *Gas* trilogy is determined not so much by the logic of individual, or group, psychology, as by the logic—we might almost say, logistics—of an idea. All of Kaiser's works are masterpieces of deduction: "To write a play," Kaiser himself suggested, "is to pursue an idea to the end."

This deliberate narrowing of the dramatic intent has its striking consequences for the form of Kaiser's plays. Where intellectual and emotional tensions are to be stated with the utmost concentration a high degree of abstraction becomes inevitable. Instead of the ample and detailed setting of the naturalistic theater, Kaiser employs few but emphatic properties in an otherwise bleak and pointedly inhuman stage space. His figures are far from the psychologically plausible characters of the realistic drama; they are, rather, nameless and puppet-like cyphers, symbols of family or class relationships who are at times distinguished only by arbitrary colors and who seem to carry the argument all the more efficiently the less specific their individuality.

The same sort of reduction to a minimum of

naturalness is characteristic of Kaiser's language: what is said by each of these schematic figures is tense and abrupt, and in syntax and vocabulary stripped of all leisurely irrelevancy. Whether we listen to the technical jargon of the engineer or to the anxious and more and more resolute voice of the "billionaire," we are always aware of that remarkable sense of direction with which Kaiser pursues his argument. The form of the dialogue is equally revealing: instead of justifying the actions of individual characters it seems rather to plot out the relay stations of the dramatic idea. This is perhaps nowhere more evident than in those passages where, for an extreme measure of antithetical speech, Kaiser resorts to the classical device of stichomythy.

Deliberate sparseness and economy of setting, figure, and language corresponds to the precision with which the play as a whole is designed. We need only analyze with some care the fourth act of *Gas I* to recognize Kaiser's craftsmanship, his use of the fugal structure, and his skill in organizing, through sound and light and a careful manipulation of group movements, a slowly rising crescendo of urgency.

Kaiser's incomparable instinct for the theatrical effect is one of his greatest assets. Indeed, it saves his plays on the one hand from becoming mere intellectual exercises in the hands of an accomplished "Denkspieler"; and on the other from that excess of exclamatory feeling which is typical of much expressionist writing. Kaiser's passion is directed toward the illumination of rational and, therefore, arguable human alternatives; his utopian vision of the "new man" is not vague and sentimental but amounts to a calculated appraisal of the energies of heart and mind and action which the human being must marshal for his own salvation. We cannot read the final speech of the "billionaire," or the second act of *Gas II*, without being moved by the superb pathos of the moralist. Here, as in the plays of Lessing or Schiller, with whom Kaiser has in form and in substance so much in common, the work of art offers us a most articulate and compelling assertion of the humanistic faith.

Victor Lange

SUGGESTED READING

Columbia Dictionary of Modern European Literature, pp. 343-345. New York, 1947.

Diebald, B. *Der Denkspieler Georg Kaiser.* Frankfurt, 1924.

Elbe, A. M. Technische und soziale Probleme in der Dramenstruktur Georg Kaisers, Diss. Cologne, 1959.

Fivian, E. A. *Georg Kaiser* (in German). Munich, 1946.

Frenz, H. "Georg Kaiser" in *Poet Lore* 1946, 363-369.

Freyhan, M. *Georg Kaisers Werk.* Berlin, 1926.

Fruchter, M. J. *The Social Dialectic in Georg Kaiser's Dramatic Works.* Philadelphia, 1933.

Kenworthy, B. J. *Georg* Kaiser, 1957.

Paulsen, W. *Georg* Kaiser, 1960.

Twentieth-Century Authors, pp. 742f. New York, 1942.

THE CORAL

CHARACTERS

The Billionaire
The Son
The Daughter
The Secretary
The Young Woman in Taffeta
The Man in Blue
The Lady in Black
The Daughter of the Lady in Black
The Gentleman in Gray
First Servant
Second Servant
The Singer
The Doctor
The Museum Director
The Captain
First Judge
Second Judge
A Guard
A Priest

The action takes place at the present day in an industralized country not definitely located.

THE CORAL
ACT ONE

An oval room, "The warm heart of the earth." Pale wall panels in which the doors are invisible, two rear, one left. Only two round armchairs of white elephant leather, center, opposite and far apart. On the outer wing of the chair right, a signal apparatus.

In this chair sits the SECRETARY. *An indefinable shy energy in the profile. Reddish stubble of hair in narrow streaks from head to chin. The frame, in its suit of the roughest material, small, yet derives weight and importance from a certain ever-ready initiative, with effort suppressed. In the other chair the* YOUNG WOMAN IN TAFFETA.

SECRETARY: Would you mind...?

THE YOUNG WOMAN IN TAFFETA: Oh, I understand you—will I be brief. I am not the only one waiting to be heard. The anteroom is crowded with others—and perhaps their cases are better justified. Who can tell? The wretched are in all the earth's corners. Whether the corner my fate thought fit to set me down in is an extra windy one ...

SECRETARY: I should have to know what your fate has been before I could judge of that.

YOUNG WOMAN IN TAFFETA: Hell, sir. Yes, hell. I do not exaggerate; that is not my way. Or might I described it better by ... one is human, sir, one has a mother ... believes in God ... yes, one is still capable of that, in spite of everything. And I can't speak the words out loud, but I ... buy my bread with my body.

SECRETARY: Do you wish to be admitted into a home?

YOUNG WOMAN IN TAFFETA: With flowers shining on the window ledges!

SECRETARY (*takes a notebook out of his pocket and writes*): You have two years' time in which to consider the foundations of a new life.

YOUNG WOMAN IN TAFFETA: Two ...

SECRETARY: The doors of every home for women who have strayed stand open to you today.

YOUNG WOMAN IN TAFFETA (*taking his hand and kissing it—hysterically*): I never sold my childhood faith. I never held God up for sale. Now he seeks me out with his messenger ... my God's messenger ... you are he. Take my burning thanks; I offer it on my knees. More than that ... more than that, it is God himself who goes amongst us again. We are all saved ... hallelujah, amen!

> (*The* SECRETARY *presses a button on the signal board. Immediately two servants enter left, herculean figures in yellow livery. They raise the* YOUNG WOMAN IN TAFFETA *and lead her through the door, rear.*)

YOUNG WOMAN IN TAFFETA (*ecstatically*): A home for the fallen—I shall become another woman there ... another ...

> (*She and the servants go. The servants admit the* MAN IN BLUE *and lead him to the chair, then go.*)

SECRETARY: Would you mind...?

MAN IN BLUE (*speaking with difficulty*): My chest ...

SECRETARY: Do you wish to be admitted to a sanatorium?

MAN IN BLUE (*burying his face in his hands*): They've turned me out now that I have worked my strength away for them. Am I an old man? No. I'm in the prime of life, but I look aged, aged. My clothes flap on my bones—once I filled them out to the very seams. The System has been the ruin of me.

SECRETARY: Are you a laborer?

Man in Blue: The System ruins everyone with its inhuman using up of all a man's capacity. And always a crowd waiting, so that one's got to be used up quick to make room for the next one.

Secretary: Can you find no employment in any factory?

Man in Blue: They don't even let me through the gates any more. I've been walking the streets for a fortnight now, and I have eaten my last penny away. Now ...

Secretary: We have settlements on the land.

Man in Blue: We have—I know. They are far off and I can't get there on foot.

Secretary: They lie on the train line.

Man in Blue: I ... haven't the price of a ticket.

Secretary (*pulls out his notebook and writes. Hands the slip of paper across*): Show this note outside.

Man in Blue (*reads—stands up*): That is more than the train fare. (*Stammering.*) I have a wife and children. I can take them with me—and I had meant to leave them!

(*The* Secretary *presses a button on the signal-board. The two servants come.*)

Man in Blue (*already hastening out, left*): My wife ... my children! (*Goes.*)

(*The servants shut the door behind him, then open it again and admit the* LADY IN BLACK *and her daughter. The* DAUGHTER *carries a violin case.*)

LADY IN BLACK (*to the servants*): Thank you—I prefer to stand. (*Servants go.*)

SECRETARY (*standing up*): Would you mind . . .?

LADY IN BLACK (*calmly*): I decided to take this step for my daughter's sake. I lost my husband a few months ago. He left me almost nothing. For myself I have been able to find a situation which will keep me, but I know that I should never earn enough for my daughter's musical training. I have reason to believe that her talent is great enough to ensure her future. I purposely brought no testimonials to that effect. The best witness to her capability is her playing. Will you hear her?

SECRETARY: I believe your daughter also will find that more enjoyable when her training is completed.

LADY IN BLACK: Am I to assume from that, that . . . (*The* SECRETARY *writes. To her daughter*): Kiss his hand.

SECRETARY (*gives the sheet to the* LADY IN BLACK): Collect this monthly until the end of her studies.

LADY IN BLACK (*without reading it*): Thanks

must weary you, you hear them so often. People must seem pitiable to you, you make so many of them happy. As for us, we can but marvel at the miracle that there can exist someone who does not shut himself away from us when we come to him with our troubles. To hear us all is an act of greater courage than the fulfillment of our requests is an act of unspeakable goodness.

> (*The* SECRETARY *presses a button on the signal board. The servants come and lead the* LADY IN BLACK *and her daughter away. A signal buzzes. Immediately the* SECRETARY *presses another button. One of the servants appears, left*).

SECRETARY: Wait. (*Servant goes.*)

> (*Through the righthand door in the rear which, as it opens, is seen to be heavily padded, the* BILLIONAIRE *hastens in. The detailed description of the* SECRETARY *above aimed at the description of the* BILLIONAIRE, *for the* SECRETARY *is merely his double, identical to a hair. Even in speech and gesture the likeness is complete.*)

BILLIONAIRE: The sailing list of the "Freedom of the Seas." Received after departure yesterday and reported this morning by radio. My son does not appear among the passengers.

SECRETARY: Only his companion.

BILLIONAIRE: The list is incomplete.

SECRETARY: They are usually perfectly accurate.

BILLIONAIRE: Where is my son if his companion is on that steamer? He must have booked on her. It was my wish. The papers published the names of every first-class passenger, and my son's was the first.

SECRETARY: I don't believe there is any error.

BILLIONAIRE: He must be on board. There is no other ship he could possibly be on. I sent express instructions to his companion that they were to come on her; she is the fastest of all steamers. The report is wrong. Get in touch with the shipping office. Ask the source of the error. Whether on board—or in the drawing-up of the list. (*Secretary hesitates.*) Wait at the telephone for an answer.

SECRETARY: It will keep me ...

BILLIONAIRE: From what?

SECRETARY: Today is Open Thursday.

BILLIONAIRE (*thoughtfully*): Open Thursday. (*The* SECRETARY *waits.*) Go and inquire. I'll stay here meanwhile. (SECRETARY *gives him the note-book.*) Say the matter is exceedingly urgent and report at once. (SECRETARY *leaves through door left.* BILLIONAIRE *sits down in chair, presses button. Serv-ants admit the* GENTLEMAN IN GRAY, *powerful frame, in ample light-gray suit, the pockets stuffed with newspapers and pamphlets, round red head, shorn. Sandals.*)

GENTLEMAN IN GRAY (*following the servants, who indicate the chair—fanning himself with his cap*): Take it slow. Wait a minute. Breathe deep. (*Servants wait.*) Better keep 'em calm out there—this is going to take some time. (*To the* BILLIONAIRE.) It won't be denied either. I shall have your attention riveted with the first three words. (*To the servants.*) I'm no wild beast. (*At a sign from the* BILLIONAIRE, *servants off.*)

BILLIONAIRE: Would you ...?

GENTLEMAN IN GRAY (*looking about him*): So this is the room all the hymns are about—fountain of great compassion—holy of holies whence love and assistance flow ... (*With descriptive gesture.*) Sweeping circle—significant form—glowing heart of the earth.

BILLIONAIRE: Say what you have to say ...

GENTLEMAN IN GRAY: Impressive bareness—two chairs—lots of room for plaints and lamentations. Extraordinary the paneling hasn't turned dark yet under the cries of distress dashing against it. (BILLIONAIRE *moves his hand toward the signal board.* GENTLEMAN *notices the movement.*) Don't ring for the servants. I know this Open Thursday is precious for all who wait. Each wasted moment and some human fate is determined.

BILLIONAIRE: In what connection do you seek my help?

GENTLEMAN IN GRAY: I ... (*leaning forward*) want to help you. (BILLIONAIRE *makes another involuntary movement toward the wall.*) No need. I'm sane, quite. I thought this over a long time. I've studied the material—worked over it—and come to the result—and the solution is of absurd simplicity. The whole struggle—this gigantic fight which is waged at present with enormous disposal of means and counter-means—collapses, flows away, is gone.

BILLIONAIRE: What struggle do you mean?

GENTLEMAN IN GRAY: The only one which rages eternally—between poor and rich.

BILLIONAIRE: That ...

GENTLEMAN IN GRAY: I can settle.

BILLIONAIRE (*with a searching look that flashes interest*): What made you come to me?

GENTLEMAN IN GRAY: You're surprised. But I had to hold your attention in the first moment or all was lost. The servants wouldn't have let me through a second time. No trifling with those two. (*Bringing out his papers with violence.*) I now proceed to develop what I briefly mentioned before. This is material—exhaustive assurances. Socialist newspapers, magazines, pamphlets, the entire arsenal of the fighting proletariat. Appeals, estimates of means for stirring up success—tariffs, statistics, tables of figures, flood of literature. Literature—nothing else. And brings nobody a single step further, the rift gapes wider every day. For it is built upon enmity to the knife. (*Pushing it all back into his pockets*.) Pity for their pains. Useless wandering in blind alleys. To no purpose. Do you follow me?

BILLIONAIRE: I don't understand.

GENTLEMAN IN GRAY: What are you doing here? Giving with both hands. Whoever asks, gets. Much or little, whatever they want. Your billions make it possible. You declare your Open Thursday. All come and receive. Wretchedness creeps over this threshold cowering, and dances out joy. The mouths of the oppressed hail paradise in this oval room—here beats the heart of the earth—glowing, merciful. Not for a moment does it miss a beat—but spends and spends. Why do you do it?

BILLIONAIRE: My millions ...

GENTLEMAN IN GRAY: No.

BILLIONAIRE: What then?

GENTLEMAN IN GRAY: Your wealth revolts you.

(BILLIONAIRE *raises one hand.*) You're not aware of it yourself, but for me there can be no other reason, I do assure you. I didn't come upon it overnight. I've run around too in all the wearisome blind alleys until I found the open road that alone leads to the goal.

BILLIONAIRE: What goal?

GENTLEMAN IN GRAY: The end of the fight, the struggle between rich and poor. A thing that no party, no parole, can bring to pass, that you can make real with a single stroke of your pen. And thereby render all the rest superfluous,—this glowing heart of the earth of yours, your Open Thursday, the assemblage of misery in your anteroom. For they are all mere drops you pour into the sea of distress. Take it from me,—I know. But by the penstroke I refer to, you can proclaim eternal peace on earth. Sign this declaration.

BILLIONAIRE (*without taking the document*): What declaration do you want of me?

GENTLEMAN IN GRAY: That you regard the enrichment of individuals as the most monstrous of evils.

BILLIONAIRE: That I ...

GENTLEMAN IN GRAY: You must. It must come from you, the billionaire of billionaires. Coming from you it will have importance, weight. Like a lightning flash it will illuminate the battlefields where the opposing forces now stand confronting each other armed to the teeth. The white flag of peaceable discussion, that is what we will run up—understanding. War will then become superfluous, the cause itself annulled. You did not desire riches—circumstances forced you. But there is a way to alter that condition, and a solution will be found and sought for in a spirit of brotherhood.

BILLIONAIRE: I hardly think...

GENTLEMAN IN GRAY: You alone, you alone can do it. You make these gifts because you have to. An inner force compels it. But it was all in little until I came to show you the greater thing—and now you will sign with joy. (*The* BILLIONAIRE *stands up.*) Surely you do not mean to call your servants?

BILLIONAIRE: I ... (*stands behind the chair thinking*).

GENTLEMAN IN GRAY: I knew you would.

BILLIONAIRE: I am going to explain to you.

GENTLEMAN IN GRAY: Your signature.

BILLIONAIRE (*again repudiating*): Then you shall say whether I am able to sign that paper or not.

GENTLEMAN IN GRAY: You must.

BILLIONAIRE (*returning to his seat*): Since it appears to be your wish to turn the whole order of things upside down, I must try to construct for you my world as it appears to me. Do you know anything of my beginnings?

GENTLEMAN IN GRAY: Yes, your own powers.

BILLIONAIRE: My own weaknesses.

(GENTLEMAN IN GRAY *looks at him disconcerted.*)

BILLIONAIRE: Or let us say—fear . . . dread. Weakness and fear, then. But you will not grasp this in the space of a word or two. My career—as they say —is told in every school book. So it is a well known story which I am about to repeat. The data will be the same, only I shall lend them a different significance. My father was an employee in the factory which now belongs to me. Whether he kept the furnace going under a cauldron or carried loads from place to place, I don't know. At any rate, he did not earn much, for we lived in wretched circumstances. One Monday—it was payday—he failed to come home. He had been given notice to quit, for he was used up—and he had taken his last money and gone off with it. He could never have provided for us any longer. On that night my mother took her own life. Somewhere in the house I heard a scream . . . I didn't run to see what it was, I knew already—I was eight years old. In that moment I knew what horror was, and it took root in me. It stood before me like a gray wall that I must climb over to escape the horror that pursued me. The horror made up of my father's staying off with his wages and my mother's scream set me on my way—drove me to flight. It stood at my back as I worked—I found employment in the same factory. It never left me even for a second—and I fled and fled before it—and flee still, for it stands behind me somewhere now as then.

GENTLEMAN IN GRAY: You made a bewilderingly rapid rise.

BILLIONAIRE: Tireless diligence, tireless industry, tireless flight, nothing else. I must keep the distance ever wider between the horror and myself. It drove me on. No hope of quarter, that much I have learned. It goaded me forward. The mind becomes ingenious against a dread that freezes up the limbs. There stood the machines which had sucked my father dry, hung my mother by the neck from a hook on a door, they would crush and maim me too unless I became their master first. The factory, with its machines—with its people set between me and the horror—that was the first I ever knew of rest.

GENTLEMAN IN GRAY (*brushing his hand across his forehead*): But after all ... such an experience occurs a hundred times a day ... the father disappears, the mother ...

BILLIONAIRE: It struck me down because I was particularly weakly. I must have been or I should have withstood it better. Instead, I ran away as hard as I could go. Have I said enough?

GENTLEMAN IN GRAY (*staggered*): I protest ...

BILLIONAIRE: Against the weakling before you?

GENTLEMAN IN GRAY: Then you have no mercy on your fellow men ...

BILLIONAIRE: No fugitive may see whom he tramples underfoot.

GENTLEMAN IN GRAY (*joyfully and with a searching regard*): Nevertheless—"The warm heart of the earth."

BILLIONAIRE: Certainly. I refuse to be brought in touch with poverty—it is too powerful a reminder. I instituted the Open Thursday, therefore—I know then when to hide myself.

GENTLEMAN IN GRAY: Yet you sit here and listen to it all.

BILLIONAIRE: Error. My Secretary sits here.

GENTLEMAN IN GRAY (*after a pause—sharply*): Is that your cosmic plan?

BILLIONAIRE: Not mine—it is *the* cosmic plan.

GENTLEMAN IN GRAY: That each class is one of the stages of escape?

BILLIONARE: All are fugitives.

GENTLEMAN IN GRAY: And the fleetest ... the ...

BILLIONAIRE: Utterest cowards ... yes ...

GENTLEMAN IN GRAY: Triumph ...

BILLIONAIRE: My sort.

GENTLEMAN IN GRAY (*groaning, then with irony*): Then I must rest my hope in a humanity without cowards.

BILLIONAIRE: Some will always be born more timid than the rest. The cause is of no consequence. It is a lever which sets itself in motion. Progress not whither but whence—your suspicions grow. Exactly. I express what you assume. And I am more familiar than you with this line of thought. Where do they come from, the great who inherit the world? They rise out of the dark because they were in the dark. And there experience the horror ... this way or that ... Blazing meteors that flare ... and fall.

GENTLEMAN IN GRAY (*mocking*): And when ... are you due to fall? (*The* BILLIONAIRE *shakes his head, smiling*.) How have you insured yourself against the fate of meteors?

BILLIONAIRE: I have a son. (*The* SECRETARY *comes back.* BILLIONAIRE *rises, goes toward* SECRETARY.) Has the mistake been corrected?

THE SECRETARY: The list was complete.

BILLIONAIRE: Without my son?

SECRETARY: He is not on the "Freedom of the Seas."

BILLIONAIRE: But his companion is.

SECRETARY: They must have separated.

BILLIONAIRE: And he with orders not to stir from his side. (*The* SECRETARY *is silent*.) I will have an explanation. At this moment I do not even know where my son is. Get into touch with his companion by radio. Let him report. Something must have happened. I do not understand how he can be traveling without my son.

SECRETARY: Your son is young.

BILLIONAIRE: Tender chains that ...? We shall soon know the reason. (SECRETARY *off again. The* BILLIONAIRE *comes back to his chair*.) Did my story affect you so deeply then?

GENTLEMAN IN GRAY (*had leapt up as the* SECRETARY *entered. He is still staring at the door through which he disappeared. Now he turns to the* BILLIONAIRE): Do I see double? Is it you sitting here? Is it you who just went through that door? Is it yourself you were just speaking to?

BILLIONAIRE: No. I was arranging a piece of business with my secretary.

GENTLEMAN IN GRAY: The secretary—! are you

brothers? But even then it would be ...

BILLIONAIRE: But possible, as you observe.

GENTLEMAN IN GRAY (*dropping into the chair*): Horrible.

BILLIONAIRE: A common prank of Nature's. You'll find a repetition of each of us, if you try, of course. I had mine looked for—and I admit that fortune favored me.

GENTLEMAN IN GRAY: Fortune—?

BILLIONAIRE: It serves many excellent purposes for me. I can be here and there without ever bestirring myself. Even at this Open Thursday I am present in my well-known person—and am perhaps on a fishing trip at some distant river.

GENTLEMAN IN GRAY: Do you still know which one you are?

BILLIONAIRE: I imagine so.

GENTLEMAN IN GRAY (*mocking*): But everybody else takes the secretary for you?

BILLIONAIRE: Except the two servants who guard my personal secretary.

GENTLEMAN IN GRAY: Otherwise you are indistinguishable?

BILLIONAIRE: Except for a small and unobtrusive sign, a coral which the secretary wears on his watch chain. The one of us who wears the coral is the secretary.

GENTLEMAN IN GRAY: And only the servants know?

BILLIONAIRE: They are detectives.

GENTLEMAN IN GRAY: What if I should betray your secret?

BILLIONAIRE: Who would believe you? It would be one more legend about me.

GENTLEMAN IN GRAY (*shaking his head energetically*): You've no coral on your watch chain—or—I didn't notice, were you wearing one before?...

BILLIONAIRE: No. I've talked to you since you came in in my own person, and if you wish to hear the rest—

GENTLEMAN IN GRAY (*laughing*): The end of your head-over-heels flight before the horror—or is there no end?

BILLIONAIRE: In my son. I have a daughter, but the stronger bond is with the son, of course. Have you children? No. Then you must allow me to know. With a son one feels his continuation—one's own continuation in his beginning. That is a law that runs in the blood. It is my most certain conviction that it is so. Every father wishes that his son shall have it better than he did.

GENTLEMAN IN GRAY: And not know the horror, as you call it.

BILLIONAIRE: Need I say any more? It is all so obvious.

GENTLEMAN IN GRAY: And have you protected him?

BILLIONAIRE: I let him live in brightness. He has no contact with those things that scream and wail from your pamphlets. I have led him along a by-path from all that.

GENTLEMAN IN GRAY: Where do you keep him hidden?

BILLIONAIRE: I don't keep him hidden. The earth has so many sunny strands.

GENTLEMAN IN GRAY: Where the horror may be dreamt away.

BILLIONAIRE: Where one can make oneself a happier past.

GENTLEMAN IN GRAY: And have rest from flight, and blessed peacefulness.

BILLIONAIRE: In paradise.

GENTLEMAN IN GRAY: You found your outward double—the secretary.

BILLIONAIRE: Does that still excite you?

GENTLEMAN IN GRAY: No, there's method in it.

BILLIONAIRE: How do you mean?

GENTLEMAN IN GRAY: And now you're forming an inward double—your son.

BILLIONAIRE: It may be my passion to exchange.

GENTLEMAN IN GRAY: With such reasons.

BILLIONAIRE: So fearsome.

GENTLEMAN IN GRAY: So powerful.

BILLIONAIRE: Do you still want to help me? With your declaration that I am to sign?

GENTLEMAN IN GRAY (*pushing his newspapers, etc., still deeper into his pockets, breathing heavily*): You've set me in a turmoil. The air's thick here. It presses the sweat out of one's paws.

BILLIONAIRE: Think it over at leisure.

GENTLEMAN IN GRAY: It is too crazy—the "Warm Heart of the Earth" ... "Open Thurdays" ... the results!

BILLLIONAIRE: What results?

GENTLEMAN IN GRAY: Chaos opens up.

BILLIONAIRE: It has already—therefore let whoever can, save himself on the first spot of firm ground he can find.

GENTLEMAN IN GRAY (*almost shouting*): Not you!

BILLIONAIRE: I have a son.

GENTLEMAN IN GRAY: Let me out of here. Buzz for your servants. I can't find the door. Buzz for them, I tell you. (*The* BILLIONAIRE *does so. The two Servants come. The* GENTLEMAN IN GRAY *threateningly to the* BILLIONAIRE) You've dashed my world to pieces—from under the ruins I curse you—I curse you. (*The Servants seize him roughly and take him out.*)

SECRETARY (*coming in again*): A radio from your son.

BILLIONAIRE: From land?

SECRETARY: No. From shipboard.

BILLIONAIRE: Is he on his way ...

SECRETARY (*reading*): "Just left ..."

BILLIONAIRE: On the "Freedom of the Seas" after all. (*The* SECRETARY *shakes his head.*) Can she have a sister ship, then, as sumptuous?

SECRETARY (*goes on reading*): "On the 'Albatross.'"

BILLIONAIRE: "Albatross"? What sort of ship is that?

SECRETARY: A coaler.

BILLIONAIRE: A ... coaler? Does he explain? (SECRETARY *hesitates—hands him a telegraph.* MILLIONAIRE *reads it through.*) A stoker ... (*collapsing against the chair*) What does it mean—my son ... on a coaler ... stoker ...?

ACT TWO

Under the awning on the deck of the BILLION-
AIRE'S *yacht. A section of the railing, rear. Heat
mist over the calm sea.*

*In white-enamelled wicker armchairs—*BILLION-
AIRE, *the* DAUGHTER, *the* MUSEUM DIRECTOR, *the*
DOCTOR, *the* CAPTAIN, *all in white. A Negro sets
out iced drinks. Off, the* SINGER'S *voice.*

SINGER (*lowering her voice on a long last note,
comes in from the rear and trains her kodak on the
group. Breaks off as she snaps*): Thanks... (*The
rest look up surprised*) for the advertisement. On
the high seas—aboard the most marvelous yacht in
the world—and such an audience! We must have
that on the record. Every opera house on earth will
compete for a contract with me. (*Dropping into a
chair beside the* BILLIONAIRE) If *you* enjoyed hearing me—or am I mistaken? Tell me the truth—I have
the picture, anyway.

BILLIONAIRE (*in some embarrassment*): No, no,
on the contrary, really extraordinary ... (*The others
clap applause.*)

SINGER (*quickly snapping again*): Second photo—the applause. (*Handing the Negro her glass*) Hot lemonade.

DOCTOR: Just what I was going to suggest to you.

SINGER: Ah, doctor, you don't know me—I'm everything, singer, impresario, and physician.

MUSEUM DIRECTOR: Then you are depriving two people of a livelihood.

SINGER: Well, isn't that the secret of success?

MUSEUM DIRECTOR: You've good healthy nerves.

SINGER: I've the most terrible nerves.

DOCTOR: Won't you explain that to me as a medical man?

SINGER: I see ghosts.

DOCTOR: What sort of ghosts?

SINGER: Just ghosts.

DOCTOR: That's more than I ever have.

SINGER: Because you haven't an excitable temperament. Artists have—that's why they see ghosts.

DOCTOR: I see. Only artists, nobody else.

SINGER: Let's ask round. It makes an entertaining game at sea. Each in turn now. (*To the* BILLIONAIRE) Do you see ghosts?

BILLIONAIRE: I'm afraid we've no time just now to ... (*To the* CAPTAIN) Isn't the "Albatross" about due to come within range now, captain?

CAPTAIN: You can't quite calculate it with ships of that type.

BILLIONAIRE: Please. (*The* CAPTAIN *goes.*)

DOCTOR: What sort of ship is this "Albatross" really?

BILLIONAIRE: My son discovered it. It must have some very special points. Most likely a yacht belonging to some friend he met on his journey.

DAUGHTER: We can challenge her to a race.

SINGER: Thrilling! What a shame I've so few films with me.

DAUGHTER: The loser to be rammed.

DOCTOR: Crew and all?

DAUGHTER: Five minutes rescue time. (*To the* BILLIONAIRE) Shall I go and tell the captain to prepare for the race?

MUSEUM DIRECTOR: Suppose the unknown "Albatross" is too much for us?

DAUGHTER: I shall stay on the bridge. I'll give the orders to the engine room, and we'll pile on all the steam we can make.

DOCTOR: At this temperature.

DAUGHTER: There'll be air up there.

DOCTOR: I was thinking of the engine room.

DAUGHTER (*stamping*): The upper deck is all I know about.

BILLIONAIRE: I don't think the "Albatross" is faster than we—so the charm of the fight isn't there.

DAUGHTER: What—my brother's chosen ship?

BILLIONAIRE: We'll leave the decision to him, then. He knows both sides. (*The* CAPTAIN *comes back.*) Sighted?

CAPTAIN: Not yet.

BILLIONAIRE (*to his daughter*): You see, she's slow. (*To the others*) Let's amuse ourselves meanwhile.

SINGER: With the ghost game—good!

BILLIONAIRE (*hastily, to the* MUSEUM DIRECTOR): Is the Tintoretto really no good at all?

MUSEUM DIRECTOR: On the contrary—it is very fine, very fine indeed.

BILLIONAIRE: But you refused it when I offered it to you.

MUSEUM DIRECTOR (*nods*): Christ carrying the cross.

SINGER: You object to the subject?

MUSEUM DIRECTOR: When I extend it to a matter of principle—yes.

DOCTOR: There'll be precious little place for old masters in your gallery in that case.

SINGER (*to the* MUSEUM DIRECTOR): Proceed with the lecture, won't you? I'll snap your audience as you arrive at the climax.

MUSEUM DIRECTOR: In the new museum I am to be the director of, my aim is to achieve a complete break with the past, however recent. I shall conduct my entire propaganda with this end in view.

DOCTOR: And what will you have left?

SINGER: Empty walls.

MUSEUM DIRECTOR: Empty walls and practically nothing to cover them.

DOCTOR: Highly original museum.

DAUGHTER: Indoor tennis courts.

MUSEUM DIRECTOR: And that very circumstance will be a spur to new productions. Emphatically a beginning. Which means especially no more disapproving criticism based on comparisons with what has gone before. We are all sitting in that shadow—in one way or another it is a source of torment to us all. We must get into the full light of things again—and shake off these cross-carryings. At least that is how I see it. It is a burden on us—a cross that we are made to carry—this mass of the past from which we can only free ourselves by acts of violence—or even crimes, if it should come to that.

DOCTOR: And do you consider it possible then—without self-deceiving?

MUSEUM DIRECTOR: I don't know.

DOCTOR: I'm afraid the cross-carrying is inevitable.

MUSEUM DIRECTOR: One must truly desire the future.

DOCTOR: You might manage it in your gallery.

MUSEUM DIRECTOR: My ambition goes no further.

DOCTOR: But in real life I doubt very much whether anyone can jump beyond his shadow.

(*A sailor comes with a report for the* CAPTAIN, *and goes.*)

CAPTAIN (*standing up.*) *To the* BILLIONAIRE): The "Albatross" is close by on the starboard side.

BILLIONAIRE (*excited*): Send the launch over. (CAPTAIN *goes.*)

DOCTOR: Now we shall know all about the mystery ship.

SINGER: And the matador.

MUSEUM DIRECTOR: My curiosity is at snapping-point.

DAUGHTER: I'm going up to flash the challenge across.

BILLIONAIRE (*holding her back. To the others*): Please go ahead; we'll come in a moment. (SINGER, MUSEUM DIRECTOR, *and* DOCTOR *go.*) I want to talk to you a second first.

DAUGHTER: Now?

BILLIONAIRE: It's only a question.

DAUGHTER: What is it?

BILLIONAIRE: Could you consider—marrying the Museum Director?

DAUGHTER: I—I don't know.

BILLIONAIRE: I want to urge you to decide, because ...

DAUGHTER: I hardly know him.

BILLIONAIRE: Nor I ...

DAUGHTER: Then how can you persuade me so?

BILLIONAIRE: I sat listening to him just now, and he impressed me as no other person ever did.

DAUGHTER: Because he rejected your gift?

BILLIONAIRE: I like his ideas. That inner independence—his philosophy which admits only the future and annihilates the past ...

DAUGHTER: I wasn't listening to him.

BILLIONAIRE: You would give me great joy ...

DAUGHTER: Then it's superfluous to ask me to think it over.

BILLIONAIRE (*shakes her hands*): Now let us go and meet your brother. (*They go.*)

> (*Sound of bells and sirens. Sailors open the railing rear and let down the companion. Everybody comes back and leans over the railing. Handkerchiefs wave. Helloes.*)

DOCTOR (*coming under the awning*): It's a clumsy old tub.

MUSEUM DIRECTOR (*following him*): Does credit to the name of "Albatross."

DOCTOR: Could you see any other passengers aboard?

MUSEUM DIRECTOR: That may have been the charm of the voyage.

DOCTOR: Thanks, not for me!

SINGER (*joins them, holding camera behind her back*): Discretion—family reunion!

> (*The* SON, *in a gray suit, comes up the stairway, and the* DAUGHTER *falls upon him with a storm of welcome. The* CAPTAIN *stands by the salute.*)

SON: Have you been lying in wait for me?

DAUGHTER: Up and down this spot for three days. Glorious bore.

BILLIONAIRE: I planned a surprise for you.

SON: Well, you've succeeded brilliantly. Your guests?

BILLIONAIRE: A few intimates, that's all.

> (*The* SON *goes from one to the other and shakes hands in silence. Then he stands beside a chair, still without a word. The awkward silence continues.*)

DAUGHTER (*flinging herself into a chair*): Bit too solemn for me.

BILLIONAIRE (*indicating the chairs*): Please. (*Everybody sits down, the* SON *last and hesitatingly. The* CAPTAIN *comes back and sits down too.*)

SON (*to him, astonished*): Aren't we going on?

BILLIONAIRE: I thought we might stay at sea another three or four days.

SON: Certainly, if you wished ...

BILLIONAIRE: On your account.

SON: What for?

BILLIONAIRE: After your travels ...

DAUGHTER: I say, I quite forgot to look at the "Albatross" in all the excitement. Is she very swell? How many knots? (*The* MUSEUM DIRECTOR *and the* DOCTOR *laugh.*)

SON: What's the matter with the "Albatross"?

DAUGHTER: We wanted to challenge her. Should we have had a good opponent?

SON: You're laughing at her. No, sister, the "Albatross" isn't an opponent at all in the way you mean.

DAUGHTER (*surprised*): Then why didn't you come on the "Freedom of the Seas"?

BILLIONAIRE (*uneasily, trying to change the subject*): Well, what about your impressions of the world's great cities?

SINGER: Did you visit the opera anywhere?

SON: We may as well define the "Albatross' " class—she's a coaler. You must know all the ships on these roads, Captain?

CAPTAIN: I'm afraid the "Albatross" had escaped me.

SON: Why? (*The* CAPTAIN *smiles. To the others*). Why should it have? Don't other people travel on such ships?

CAPTAIN: They are not arranged for passengers.

SON: No, not for passengers. But what about the sailors. Aren't stokers people?

MUSEUM DIRECTOR (*after a pause*): You understand the refinements of pleasure.

SON: What pleasure?

MUSEUM DIRECTOR: It is the antithesis between the coaler and this yacht that enables you to savor its luxury as never before.

SON: Or else to—(*breaking off, and turning to the* BILLIONAIRE) Did you have a report from my companion?

BILLIONAIRE: I did not speak to him.

SON: But he must have got back two days ago.

BILLIONAIRE: I've been lying out here for two days.

SON: Are you displeased with him? I take all the blame. He did all he could to prevent it.

BILLIONAIRE (*avoiding the subject*): Won't you change your clothes?

DAUGHTER: That's a city suit you have on.

SON: It's a better protection against the coal dust whirling about. And besides it was less noticeable— it's wiser to be part of the picture.

BILLIONAIRE: Do so then—go and get into white from head to foot like us.

SON: Please let me enjoy myself my own way.

SINGER (*busy with the camera*): Most interesting pictorial effect.

SON: Is that the only way it strikes you?

DOCTOR: In this extreme heat white clothing is a matter of health.

BILLIONAIRE: There spoke our careful doctor— obey him.

SON (*with repressed sharpness*): Would you expect your professional advice to be followed in the engine room too?

DOCTOR: Scarcely.

SON: Because you don't enforce it there. Because of the black coal they work with.

DOCTOR: Exactly.

SON: Therefore health down there must suffer,

while up here it must be taken care of?

MUSEUM DIRECTOR: You seem to have seen more things on your tour than you ...

SON: When it is the first trip, one keeps one's eyes wide open.

DAUGHTER: Did you meet any princes?

SINGER: Tell us all about it.

SON: Every day.

DAUGHTER: Have you made any friends? Is anyone coming to visit you soon?

SON: I could introduce five—ten—to you off my coaler. Come with me next time.

MUSEUM DIRECTOR: Is this another ...

SON: Refinement of pleasure?

> (*A sailor comes with a report to the* CAPTAIN. *The* CAPTAIN *goes to the* DOCTOR *and whispers to him. They go.*)

SON: Aren't we going on now?

BILLIONAIRE: I have given no orders.

SON: What did the doctor go off with the captain for?

SINGER: One of the crew's had an accident, I expect.

SON: Wouldn't you like to take a snapshot of it?

DAUGHTER: We might as well start moving—it would be one way of getting some air. This heat is really becoming unbearable.

SON: And we're on deck.

SINGER: Is it cooler anywhere else?

SON: No—hotter.

SINGER: Not possible!

SON: Go below into the stokehole.

BILLIONAIRE: Let's start going.

MUSEUM DIRECTOR (*ironically*): Mind the stokers.

SON: Do you know what it means to be by those furnaces?

MUSEUM DIRECTOR: I have never sought the opportunity to try it.

SON: And a description would hardly interest you.

MUSEUM DIRECTOR: Oh, graphically done by an expert . . .

SON: I am an expert!

BILLIONAIRE (*to the* DAUGHTER): Please go and tell the captain . . .

DAUGHTER: Full steam ahead!

SINGER: The ladies take over the command.

DAUGHTER: Here's where we make a new record. We'll radio it to the papers tonight and tomorrow the whole world will burst with envy. (*Goes off.*)

SON: Won't you stop that wickedness?

BILLIONAIRE: The yacht has never shown her full

capacity yet.

Son: Then I must ask you to drop me first.

Museum Director: The coaler has unaccustomed you to speed.

Son: No, to frivolity, perhaps.

Billionaire: You need to enjoy that sort of sport.

Son: I am ashamed to have come to a right mind so late.

Billionaire: What does that mean?

Son: That I ... (*reflecting*) if I'm to take part in this record-making, I can only do it before the boilers.

Billionaire (*to the* Museum Director): Don't keep the ladies waiting on the bridge. (*The* Museum Director *goes. To his* Son, *slowly*) Did you really travel on that ship as a stoker?

Son: I couldn't hold out under it, so I had to become a passenger again.

Billionaire: Did it specially attract you to ...?

Son: Oh, the steamer is the least important part of it.

Billionaire: You saw much to wonder at in your travels.

Son: It was as though scales fell from my eyes. The wrongs we are committing stood up clearly before me. We rich here—and there the others, strangling in want and misery—but people like ourselves. There's not a spark of right in it—why do we do it? I ask you why? Give me an answer that absolves us both, you and me.

BILLIONAIRE (*staring at him.*): You ask me?

SON: Yes, and I shall never stop asking you. I have never been so grateful to you as now, never in my life. You gave me that trip, and but for it I should have stayed blind to the end of my days.

BILLIONAIRE: You will forget.

SON: Forget what is in me now, and fills me through and through? That will only disappear when I disappear too.

BILLIONAIRE: What is in you?

SON: The horror of that life which I have seen, with its toil and oppression.

BILLIONAIRE: Travel experiences are not enough to ...

SON: Not enough?

BILLIONAIRE: You exaggerate superficial impressions.

SON: They burn in my blood. And the vividest picture of all is the "Freedom of the Seas" as she lay in her wharf. Flags, music, passengers in light clothes strolling up and down the decks, chattering, gay. And a few yards underneath their feet, hell. Men feeding fire-belching holes, quivering bodies burning to death. So that we may make speed, speed. I had started to sail on that ship, I had set my foot on her deck—but I had to turn back—and only on that "Albatross" I began to feel my conscience lighter.

BILLIONAIRE: And have you conquered all that now?

SON: Now I feel it more than ever. Here on this wonderful private yacht of yours. I feel the blood beating in my heart with shame. Look at us lying back in these chairs in indolence, wailing about the heat the sun pours down on us. We sip iced water for ease, and not a grain of dust irritates our throats. And underneath the soft soles of your white shoes here, there are men with boiling fever in their veins. Tear away this wall of wooden planks—see how thin it is, but yet how fearfully it divides—and look down, look down, all of you. And the words will stick in your mouths before any of you will brag before one of them down there. (*The* DOCTOR *strolls in.*)

SON (*springing toward him*): What was it, doctor?

DOCTOR: A yellow stoker collapsed.

SON: Dead?

Doctor (*shaking his head*): Heatstroke.

Son: Where have you put him?

Doctor: I had him laid in front of a ventilator shaft.

Son: Not brought up here?

Doctor: No.

Son (*briefly*): Wait here. (*He goes.*)

Doctor (*drops into a chair. To the* Negro): Ice water. (*To the* Billionaire) I find this long drifting at sea extraordinarily quieting to the nerves. I'd like to prescribe it for you five days every other month. (Billionaire *does not move.*) I promise myself success with this new diet I've put you on. (Billionaire *silent.*) Of course we can't offer you the keen and healthful excitement of meeting your son again, but your daughter will be able to invent surprises of a more moderate kind for you. I'll talk to her about it. (*Voices and footsteps approach. The* Doctor *puts down his glass.*) Are they playing deck games? (Sailors *bring the half-naked yellow stoker.*)

Son: This way.

Doctor (*standing up*): What does this mean?

Son: Set two chairs together. Take hold, doctor, this is a life and death matter. (*To the* Sailors). Lay him down. (*To the* Negro). *Ice water.* (*To the*

Doctor) Come over here, doctor, you understand this better than I. Wash his chest. (*To the* BILLIONAIRE) Will you allow your personal physician to lend a hand? (*To the* DOCTOR) Is it dangerous?

CAPTAIN (*coming in—low, to* BILLIONAIRE): I couldn't prevent him.

(*The* BILLIONAIRE *shakes his head decidely.*
The DAUGHTER *and the* SINGER *come in.*)

SON (*to the* DAUGHTER): Won't you help us here, sister? A man may be dying. (*The* DAUGHTER *goes nearer.*) Wet your hands in that ice water and lay them on his hot chest. I am only calling you to your simple duty. (*The* DAUGHTER *does so. To the* DOCTOR, *beside himself*) Doctor, save him—you've got to, or I am a murderer!

BILLIONAIRE (*stares down at the group—his lips move—at last he mutters*): The horror!

SINGER (*focusing her camera—to the* MUSEUM DIRECTOR): I've never had pictures like these before. (*She snaps.*)

ACT THREE

Square room with rear wall of glass—the BILLION-AIRE'S *workroom. Right and left on the walls, from the floor to the ceiling, huge brown-toned photographs of factories. Broad desk with swivel chair; another chair at the side. Smokestacks outside, close and straight like pillars of dead lava holding up cloud mountains of smoke.*

BILLIONAIRE (*at the desk*): How many dead?

SECRETARY (*standing by the desk*): The exact number of victims could not be ascertained, for the men who were saved and brought into the light rushed away and had not reported yesterday.

BILLIONAIRE: What did they do that for?

SECRETARY: They must have experienced untold horror the three days they were shut up under the ground.

BILLIONAIRE: And now they flee from it, farther and farther?

SECRETARY: They came up distracted as if from their graves, screaming and shuddering.

BILLIONAIRE: Whoever is absent from his place

by the day after tomorrow will not be taken back again.

Secretary (*making a note*): By the day after tomorrow.

Billionaire: How did the meeting go? Was I contradicted? Was I allowed to speak without interruption?

Secretary: No.

Billionaire: Was my life in danger?

Secretary: It was indeed.

Billionaire: How did I protect myself?

Secretary: I had requisitioned troops. They were lined up before me ready to shoot.

Billionaire: Did anything happen?

Secretary: Only one man kept yelling interruptions.

Billionaire: What did he say?

Secretary: "Murderer."

Billionaire: Was he not to be found?

Secretary: The crowd covered him.

Billionaire: Let him be found. Threaten to take steps if he is not delivered. (*The* Secretary *makes a note.*) Is everything quiet now?

Secretary: The shaft is being worked again today.

Billionaire: What means did I use?

SECRETARY: I announced the shutting down of the entire works.

BILLIONAIRE: Thanks. (*A green lamp lights on the desk.* BILLIONAIRE *takes up the receiver. Surprised*): Who? ... My daughter? ... Here? ... Yes, I will see her. (*To the* SECRETARY) Replace me in Factory 24. There has been an explosion there—I said I would be down during the afternoon. (*The* SECRETARY *makes a note.*) Thanks. (*The* SECRETARY *leaves, left, through an invisible door. The* BILLIONAIRE *stands up, makes a few rapid steps toward the wall right, changes his mind, returns to his chair and plunges into his work. One of the Servants opens a padded invisible door. The* DAUGHTER *enters.* SERVANT *goes. The* BILLIONAIRE *looks round.*) Your first visit to your father's business house.

DAUGHTER (*looking about*): Yes—I am seeing it for the first time.

BILLIONAIRE: Another world! ... Is the matter so urgent that you couldn't keep it until this evening before the fire?

DAUGHTER: I can only explain it to you here.

BILLIONAIRE: Am I to prepare myself for the most joyful news?

DAUGHTER: What is that?

BILLIONAIRE: I asked something of you that day

we were waiting for your brother ... On the yacht.

Daughter (*shaking her head*): I have never given that another thought.

Billionaire (*suppressing his uneasiness. Gaily*): Really not?

Daughter: It was on the yacht that I first saw my way.

Billionaire: To your brightest happiness?

Daughter: To my inevitable duty.

Billionaire (*lifts his hand high in protest*): Not that!

Daughter (*calmly*): When I took my hands from the seething breast of that yellow stoker they were marked. The scar sank into my blood, into my deepest heart. I have no choice. I feel the call. And submit to it willingly. You will show me the place where I shall best obey it.

Billionaire: What do you want to do?

Daughter: Send me where the suffering is worst, to the injured in your factories. I will nurse them.

Billionaire: You don't know what you are saying.

Daughter: I do. You can at least respect my action by believing it. I want to go to the shaft where the catastrophe happened.

Billionaire: What catastrophe?

DAUGHTER: You put down the agitation yourself.

BILLIONAIRE: Who carries you these tales?

DAUGHTER: Reports in the papers are forbidden. Yes, I know you are powerful.

BILLIONAIRE (*stares at her. A pause*): Let it be. (*He get up and goes to her.*) I shall not ask you with words. You have a hundred to every one of mine. It is an unequal fight between father and daughter. The end is a foregone conclusion. (*He takes her hands, looks intently at her.*) No ... no. Such little hands ... such weak hands. (*He anticipates her contradiction with a shake of the head.*) Yes, yes ... strong and hard. And only I know what for—to storm fortresses, to heap up ruins, and the victims under them. Shall I tell you who the victim is?

DAUGHTER: Now I don't understand you.

BILLIONAIRE: Do you want to make me your victim? (DAUGHTER *looks at him wonderingly.*) Then turn back. You will find your task lies nearer home. Does it seem a paltry one to you? It seems important to me because it concerns your father.

DAUGHTER (*drawing her hands away*): I have no right, while others ...

BILLLIONAIRE: Father and Daughter ... not by quarrelling! Only by asking and yielding.

DAUGHTER: I thank you today for the lovely years of youth ...

BILLIONAIRE: And as lovely a future.

DAUGHTER (*strongly*): Which will be a shining memory through my new life of duty. (*She stands up and puts out her hand.*) My decision was made so easily. Would you make it hard for me by having me change it?

BILLIONAIRE (*without taking her hand*): Where are you going now?

DAUGHTER: To my sisters and brothers.

BILLIONAIRE (*in a dead voice*): So that's where you're going ...

DAUGHTER: Will you still know me among the poorest of the poor?

BILLIONAIRE (*supporting himself against the desk*): You're going there ... (*The* DAUGHTER *hesitates ... turns to the door. The* SERVANT *opens.* DAUGHTER *goes. The* BILLIONAIRE *falters ... makes a timid gesture.*) There ... there ... there ... (*Then pulls himself together and rings. The* SECRETARY *enters.*) Shut down the shaft. (*The* SECRETARY *makes a note.*) No! (*Clutching his brow*) It's here or there ... it can't be blown away ... no one has power to do that! (*Firmly to the* SECRETARY) My daughter wishes to dedicate herself to Samaritan work. You will meet her at the shaft and wherever accidents occur in my factories. Repudiate her ... I know my daughter no longer.

SECRETARY: Does your daughter know about the coral?

BILLIONAIRE: No; besides the two servants, nobody knows. (*Businesslike again*) We were interrupted ...

SECRETARY (*reads from his notebook*): In the afternoon I represent you at Factory 24.

BILLIONAIRE: Tomorrow at noon I shall attend the first half of the Missions meeting myself; I am to be appointed honorary president. Come in the car at two. Under the pretext of fetching something I shall leave the hall. You return in my place and read my contribution to them. I'll give you the papers. (*He looks in a drawer of the desk. The green lamp flashes*).

SECRETARY: Telephone. (*The* BILLIONAIRE *springs up—stares at the lamp.*) I'll come back later to ...

BILLIONAIRE (*brusquely*): Stay here! ... Go now. Yes ... later. (*The* SECRETARY *goes. The* BILLIONAIRE *takes the receiver up slowly.*) Who ... (*He lets it fall from his slack fingers onto the deck. His mouth quivers.*) My son ... (*The* SERVANT *admits the* SON *and goes. The* BILLIONAIRE *stiffly erect goes toward him.*) I have not seen you the last few days.

SON: Since ...

BILLIONAIRE: I am not asking where you were. The time is past for me to keep watch over your comings and goings. You must justify your actions to yourself now. You are grown up.

SON: You make it easy for me ...

BILLIONAIRE: Perhaps it was important to tell you this. Is that what you came for?

SON: The reason ...

BILLIONAIRE: I will not probe into you to find it out. Sit down. In this stern work-a-day room ...

SON: Which you have always jealously kept me out of ...

BILLIONAIRE: Is it your ambition to see yourself in my place?

SON: Not in yours.

BILLIONAIRE: I'll not offer it to you. I'm not tired yet. The strings are still taut in my fingers. I shall, and can, go on working. The successor arrives too early. You shall not dethrone me today, nor tomorrow either.

SON: That was not my intention.

BILLIONAIRE: It would help you to prepare your life accordingly.

50

Son: You narrow the field.

Billionaire: It is your only chance. The work is my share.

Son: I know how you mean to go on.

Billionaire: You see, the gates are well barred.

Son: I stand compelled, and therefore I must pacify my conscience.

Billionaire: A compulsion lies on you too.

Son (*after a pause*): Will you answer certain questions that burn in me like fire?

Billionaire: If our boundaries are sharply drawn and understood—yes.

Son: Such deep contradictions split all your dealings.

Billionaire: Do you concern yourself with me?

Son: I can concern myself with nothing else.

Billionaire: What has made me so unexpectedly interesting?

Son: This monstrous wealth that you have assembled ...

Billionaire: I have already mentioned my working powers.

Son: That is not working power, it is ...

Billionaire: Wherein lies the riddle?

Son: Here the ruthless profits ... and there the limitless charity that you give. The "Warm Heart of the Earth" . . . and the stone that you must bear in your inmost soul.

BILLIONAIRE: I don't want to solve that riddle for you.

SON: Because shame of confessing it holds you back.

BILLIONAIRE: It shall remain my secret.

SON: I tear at the veil you hide behind. You know your wealth is a mortal sin, and stifle knowledge with your "Open Thursday."

BILLIONAIRE: The explanation would not suffice.

SON: No, these gifts of yours are absurd, ridiculous. You can't pay that way for the blood . . .

BILLIONAIRE: I shed?

SON: No, those are accidents. But you threaten with bloodshed when they dare to cry out.

BILLIONAIRE: Did you see that?

SON: Now I must confess what it nearly drove me to yesterday.

BILLIONAIRE: Why yesterday?

SON: I was at the shaft while you were speaking. You had to appear there yourself to put down that uprising. I was down below in that haggard crowd— and saw you standing there behind the menacing guns. So cold and far away. Your words cracked down upon the gathering like bits of ice. No one dared to lift his voice again. Until you said the works would be shut down, and thousands—children and women—delivered up to hunger. That tore one mouth open.

BILLIONAIRE: So it was you ...

SON: Cried out "murder!"—And that was not the last.

BILLIONAIRE: It was the last I heard.

SON: Could I have but forgotten that it was my father standing up there—(*He reaches into his pocket, then lays a revolver on the table.*) I do not wish to be tempted twice.

BILLIONAIRE (*shoves the gun aside*): You wouldn't have hit me.

SON: I meant to try it.

BILLIONAIRE (*shaking his head and smiling*): No, not me. So this need not stand as a shadow between us two. (*He puts out his hand.*) Don't let it bother you.

SON (*staring at him*): Do you puff it away like a grain of dust on your coat?

BILLIONAIRE: Not *my* coat.

SON: Forget and forgive?

BILLIONAIRE: So there was nothing to forgive.

SON: No, not for you. No one else can do that. Not that. One allots one's own atonement. And I will make mine so heavy that maybe on my dying day I shall dare to raise my eyes again.

BILLIONAIRE: To me?

SON: No, you've taken me back today. You've got no time to waste.

BILLIONAIRE: Then whom do you set over you as judge?

SON: The least of your workmen.

BILLIONAIRE: What does that mean?

SON: Until another's despair drives him to the same, I shall stand down there with them.

BILLIONAIRE: In the uprising?

SON: In the peace that will be spread around if I become one with them all, and no more than the least of them.

BILLIONAIRE (*pushes the revolver toward him*). The time is now. (*He turns his face away.*)

SON (*jumps and runs to him*): Oh, tell me why all this should be—tell me why.

BILLIONAIRE: Come. (*He leads him to the photographs.*) See there? Gray factories. Narrow yards. (*Crossing to the great window, rear*) Do you see that? Where is the earth here—grass blades—bushes —? From such as this I came ... Do you know my life? I have kept it hidden from you. But it is read in all the schools. I had another life for you to live, and I have let you live it. Yours, not mine. . . I came up out of nothing, so the books say. . . I swung myself up out of that very poverty here—I tell you this now. And I have never forgotten it. Not for a single hour have I allowed myself to drowse. I set these pictures about me—I made this wall of glass so that none of that might be hidden—it was to goad me into wakefulness should I ever fall weary and seek to rest. It was for warning and admonition in my blood—only not down again—not down again to that.

Son (*withdrawing from him*): You . . .

Billionaire: I can warn you, you'll believe me. It swallowed up my father and my mother. Its arm was already grasping after me—but I escaped.

Son: You know . . .

Billionaire: A single moment upset you. I have shuddered before it for a lifetime. So terrible is life. . . . Do you wish to go down there?

Son: You tear the very last thing out of my hands. . . .

Billionaire: What is that?

Son: My only excuse for you—that never having known, you could not grasp the suffering of others.

Billionaire: I bear the cry within my breast.

Son: Are you a tiger? Worse, for the tiger knows

not what he does. You know the torture of your victims ... and. ... (*He grasps the gun, but lays it
down again.*)

BILLIONAIRE: I or another ...

SON: Everyone is ...

BILLIONAIRE: Be thankful to me.

SON: For this?

BILLIONAIRE: That you need never be who I am.

SON (*calmly*): Your blood is mine ...

BILLIONAIRE: Do you feel it too?

SON: It makes the task worth while.

BILLIONAIRE: Of saving me from the pursuing
horror?

SON: Of stifling these terrible desires, and holding
steadfast by the side of the humblest of your em-
ployees. (BILLIONAIRE *stands stiffly.*) You can't
prevent it. I shall take work wherever I can find it.

BILLIONAIRE (*collapsing at his feet*): Mercy ...
mercy! !

SON (*coldly*): Upon whom?

BILLIONAIRE: Mercy! ...

SON: And that may be my cry to you on the day
you deny me and my comrades bread. (*Before the*
SERVANTS *have the door fully open, he is gone,
right.*)

BILLIONAIRE (*bounding up at last. He looks for*

the revolver and thrusts it into his pocket): Not here ... in the heart of the woods. Green bowers for the glazing eyes, a bit of blue heaven fluttering down, tinkle of little birds. (*Glancing sideways at the walls*) Stopped? Cut off? ... Failed in the flight? ... Overtaken? ... (*Swinging his arms about*) Let me go! ... Don't touch me! ... With a child's terror I fear you, all of you! (*He runs around the line of photographs, panting, beating upon them with his hands.*) A way out.... A way out ... (*Screaming*) A way out! (SECRETARY *enters from left. Looks questioningly.* BILLIONAIRE *stares at him*).

SECRETARY (*embarrassed*): You're papers? (*The* BILLIONAIRE *is silent.*) You wish to give me some papers?

BILLIONAIRE (*staggering to the desk and collapsing in a chair*): Daughter and son ... down ... down. My children have deserted me. (SECRETARY *silent.* BILLIONAIRE *glances up at him.*) Do you understand what it means to have worked for your children all your life long—and then to have them come to you, their father, and knock the whole thing out of your hands?

SECRETARY: Your son?

BILLIONAIRE (*crying out*): Who will help now to

pull down mountains—to cover this? (*The* Secretary *looks at him inquiringly.*) Will no one help me
now out of the darkness of my past?

Secretary: Your achievements are so gigantic,
your past needs no embellishment.

Billionaire: No? ...

Secretary: Your work stands out the greater
for it.

Billionaire: I give it up—I'll pay with all my
riches—I'll give my life in exchange for any other
man's. (*Full of deep feeling*) Who'll lend me a life
that was bright from its first days on? In my son I
can find that no more—down... Where is the exchange I have longed for and wooed in the fever of
work and the rage for possession—on the heights
of my mountainous riches? ... In whom can I now
sink myself and lose this fear, this turmoil that
destroy me? Whose life—smooth and good life—for
mine?

Secretary (*looking down at him with growing
emotion*): Your son has chosen another way. No
disappointment is bitterer. But as it repeats itself so
many thousandfold, it is as if it were a law. Father
and son strive away from each other. It is always a
struggle of life and death. (*Pause.*) I opposed my
father too, and although I felt the hurt it was to

him, yet I was forced to hurt him. ... (*After another pause*) I don't know yet what it was that drove me to it. The desire to try out life myself—perhaps it was that. The need to stand alone is stronger than everything else. (*With heightened animation*) There are few homes like mine. I have a wonderful youth to look back upon. I was an only son. Mother and father lavished an infinite treasure of love upon me. And in the shelter of their care I saw and heard nothing of the wretchedness and irritations of everyday. Sunlight lay on all our quiet rooms. Even death passed us by. My parents—even today, they still live only for me. Then I passed into the little university, and the urge for independence began to possess me. I broke away and went into the world. ... I have been through many a dark hour. Buffeted here and there—but deep down nothing could shake me, for I possessed the greatest riches of all, endless and inexhaustible—the living memory of a happy childhood. Whatever might come later could be only waves upon the surface of a lake whose clearness mirrored the blue of heaven. So untroubled, so calm, within me lies that perfect past.

> (*The* Billionaire *has raised his face toward him. He listens with deepest intentness. The*

SECRETARY *gazes into space.*)

BILLIONAIRE (*looking about the table*): The papers. (SECRETARY *gives them to him. He speaks with a great effort.*) Go. (*The* SECRETARY *takes the papers, turns to the door. The* BILLIONAIRE *pulls the revolver out of his pocket and presses the trigger. His* SECRETARY, *shot through the back, falls. The* BILLIONAIRE *stands immobile.*) My life—for another's . . . that was bright . . . from the first day on . . . (*Goes slowly forward to the body and bends down . . . slips the coral off the watch chain. Holds it before him on his open palm.*) This is the life I thirst for . . . every day of this life. . . . I covet and long for. (*Flings back his head.*) Those bright days shall make me happy. . . . (*He slips the coral on his watch chain. Then wrenches open the door and shoots again into the air. The two* SERVANTS *rush in. One remains in the doorway standing—the other bends over the* SECRETARY.)

FIRST SERVANT (*in the doorway*): The coral?

SECOND SERVANT (*kneeling upright, shaking his head.*) Arrest the Secretary.

ACT FOUR

Room of examining magistrates—blue square with many entrances by iron-barred doors behind which narrow passages lose themselves. A hanging lamp of clear glass lights the place brightly. One small iron table at which the clerk—with eye shade—is seated.

The FIRST JUDGE *is standing in an attitude of reflection. The two* SERVANTS, *left.* GUARD *comes in, right.*

FIRST JUDGE: Put the light out.

> (GUARD *strides to switchboard, the lamp goes out. Frosted lamps glow in the corners.*)

FIRST JUDGE (*goes to the table and takes up the receiver*): Relief, please. (*To the* SERVANTS) You may now . . . (*on second thoughts*) Or wait another minute or two. (*He has the clerk give him the dossier, reads, shakes his head. To the* SERVANTS) Did the secretary ever allow the coral to . . . (*Quickly*) It is possible that the coral had been exchanged *for* once, to . . . (*The* SECOND JUDGE *comes in, rear.*)

SECOND JUDGE: No result.

FIRST JUDGE (*gives him the papers*): Nothing more than that I now have certain doubts.

SECOND JUDGE: There's something like genius in the consistency with which he persists in masking his person.

FIRST JUDGE: His silence is certainly consistent enough.

SECOND JUDGE: He does not respond to the most obvious inquiries as to his earlier life—after all the foundation of every examination. But he receives them all as though he himself did not know. We have had to gather the data all ourselves.

FIRST JUDGE: Yes, it seems as unknown to him as though he heard of his own life today for the first time.

SECOND JUDGE: Is he simply leading us on? . . .

FIRST JUDGE: What do you mean by that?

SECOND JUDGE: Are we to preach his past to him?

FIRST JUDGE: To what end?

SECOND JUDGE: To wear us out.

FIRST JUDGE: He's almost done that to me already.

SECOND JUDGE (*reads—lets the sheet fall*): He does not argue the point about the coral having been found on him.

FIRST JUDGE: But he refuses to admit he's the secretary.

SECOND JUDGE: Then how does he explain the coral on his watch chain? (*Reading*) "This repeated question the prisoner consistently refuses to answer."

FIRST JUDGE (*to* SERVANTS): Was there never a plan to confuse you in the same connection for certain purposes?

FIRST SERVANT: No. Our task would have been impossible if there had been.

SECOND SERVANT: The murdered man set great store by the personal watch he set over his person.

SECOND JUDGE: It's perfectly transparent to me. Of course, it's a matter of the fellow's neck. That's a thing one rather jibs at. But we have the son's affidavit. In the conversation that had taken place just before between father and son, the son renounced his father's riches. The daughter renounced it too. The secretary had heard the excited talk next door and could not withstand the temptation to make himself their successor. So he made no bones about it and went ahead. Only the coral he hadn't time to exchange, though he would have liked to. (*To the* SERVANTS) The shot brought you there at once.

SECOND SERVANT: I got him as he was trying to make it out of the door.

SECOND JUDGE: Did he try to get away?

FIRST SERVANT: We didn't open the door—he did.

FIRST JUDGE: Why should he run away when he gives himself out for the one who was attacked?

SECOND JUDGE (*puts the dossier down*): That very attempt at flight proves it. The report made more noise than he had reckoned with. He was bewildered and expected to get away, but the plan was knocked to pieces by the servants' watchfulness. Now he has to recall the part he first meant to play.

FIRST JUDGE: But the resemblance is extraordinary, anyway. I've never experienced such a case of doubles.

SECOND JUDGE: Yes, if it weren't for the coral, we should be groping in the dark and never find a way out. (*Seizing the papers*) Besides, how does he account for the attack which is alleged to have been made by the secretary?

FIRST JUDGE: He says nothing.

SECOND JUDGE: Because there never was such an attack.

FIRST JUDGE: But you said he wished to put himself in the murdered man's place.

SECOND JUDGE (*wavers*): So that would be a reason, wouldn't it?

SECOND JUDGE: To prompt him to kill.

FIRST JUDGE: So he acted under stress.

SECOND JUDGE (*excited*): But he is the secretary.

FIRST JUDGE (*rubbing his eyes*): I am really worn out. The sharp light—the passiveness of that man who hardly bothers to defend himself—

SECOND JUDGE: I am thinking of disposing of certain means to make him more active. If showing him the coral has no effect ... (*He picks it up from the table.*) The thing looks like a drop of blood still hanging onto the murderer. ... (*He lays it down. To the* SERVANTS) I don't need you any longer.

FIRST SERVANT: What time tomorrow?

SECOND JUDGE: Let's hope this is the last. Ten times over the same litany. If you're needed, I'll send for you. (*They go.*)

FIRST JUDGE: Do you promise yourself better success tonight?

SECOND JUDGE: Nothing more than a full confession.

FIRST JUDGE (*taken aback*): How do you expect to bring him to that?

SECOND JUDGE: He insists he's the billionaire. Very well, I'll bring his children to face him. Now nature can be the judge. If he hesitates a single moment to approach them—for we know by their own testimony that he loved his son and daughter above everything—then he has as good as confessed. He can face the coral—it's a dead object—but before the weight of his victim's son's and daughter's eyes nobody could stand up. And as he is no professional criminal, I'll have him break down like a straw.

FIRST JUDGE: Honestly, I'm completely played out.

SECOND JUDGE: Stretch out on the sofa and have a good sleep. If you don't mind my disturbing you, I'll shout the news of our deliverance from this fortnight's martyrdom across to you.

FIRST JUDGE: I'll go straight to the country for a week.

SECOND JUDGE: And I'll write a book about the case—popular edition of several hundred thousand! (FIRST JUDGE *goes off.* SECOND JUDGE *goes toward left and rings a bell beside a door. Led in by a* GUARD, *the* SON *and* DAUGHTER *in black—left.*) It is after all necessary that I bring you actually to confront the man. Gladly as I would have spared you this painful experience, the obstinate denial which my colleague has been unable to break down in him forces me to this step. I see no other way to get a confession out of him. And we must have the confession absolutely.

SON: Instruct us how we are to behave.

SECOND JUDGE: I intend to deal a surprise blow. He must not be allowed the least time for reflection. I must ask you to come absolutely noiselessly and not in any way to betray your presence here. For the present wait there in the back of the corridor—the guard stands round about the door. That won't strike him as peculiar. (*To* GUARD) During the hearing I shall arrange to come this side so that the prisoner will have his back to your door. As soon as I pull out my handkerchief, admit the lady and gentleman.

SON: Is our task over when we have confronted him?

SECOND JUDGE: Obviously, I shall see that it last no longer than it must. But try to look at him intently. That is important. Especially you, madam, I should like to impress this upon. Take hold of yourself. You are about to experience the most horrible thing one could well encounter. You will think you are looking at your father who is dead.

SON: But some distinction must be possible.

SECOND JUDGE: We should have had it easy, then. The resemblance is complete. No bodily mark exists. Nature has played this trick on us.

SON: Only the coral can decide?

SECOND JUDGE: And irrevocably. Therefore do

not forget that you have the secretary before you. (SON *and* DAUGHTER *off left with the* GUARD. *The* GUARD *comes back and waits behind the iron-barred door. To the* FIRST GUARD) Bring him in. (*The* GUARD *switches on the light. Off right* SECOND JUDGE *puts on blue-glass spectacles.* GUARD *lets the* BILLIONAIRE *precede him into the room and remains at the door. His hands are bound in front of him with thin steel rope. He prepares to stand as he is now accustomed to do—without a sign of excitement.* SECOND JUDGE *for the moment does not notice him. Then he takes the revolver from the table and goes—merely interested in the weapon—to the* BILLIONAIRE.) Where do you buy this make? (BILLIONAIRE *is silent.*) I'd like one myself. But I can't very well pinch one that the law has confiscated. (BILLIONAIRE *smiles thinly.*) A close-kept secret?

BILLIONAIRE: A present.

SECOND JUDGE: Indeed? Who from? (BILLIONAIRE *shakes his head.*) Surely from no tender hand.

BILLIONAIRE: From the tenderest.

SECOND JUDGE: Oh, come, that is unnatural.

BILLIONAIRE: Yes—it was unnatural.

SECOND JUDGE: Was it for you to use on yourself if ever you should be untrue?

BILLIONAIRE: I was the target.

SECOND JUDGE: Who wanted to shoot you? (BILLIONAIRE *slowly nods his head.*) Did you tear the weapon out of his hand?

BILLIONAIRE: He put it down on the desk.

SECOND JUDGE (*quickly*): The billionaire? (BILLIONAIRE *silent. The* SECOND JUDGE *nods with relief and goes to the right.*) Let's reconstruct the situation. Turn towards me. (BILLIONAIRE *does so.*) Wait a bit. The metal's got a bit dull—it must have shone rather before. (*He pulls out his handkerchief and rubs it. The* GUARD, *left, moves back from the door.*)

SECOND JUDGE: Of course it's all poppycock about the gun lying about on the table. In fact your whole story is so completely muddled that there's no use trying to grope for sense in it any more. The long and short of the matter is this: under some pretext or other you got behind your victim's back, pulled the gun out of your trousers pocket, and stood all set and ready, exactly as you see me standing now, with this same distance between you— (*The* GUARD *has come in with the* SON *and* DAUGHTER. *They stand waiting.*) Turn your back!

THE BILLIONAIRE (*turns around. Without hesitation he goes toward his* SON *and* DAUGHTER): Children! In black! Has there been a death—close to us? You wonder why I don't know of it. I am out of touch with you all for the present, locked up under the strictest watch. An intolerable error that must be cleared up first. I am all imaginable pains to destroy this dreadful suspicion. But the courts are conscientious. Every trifle has weight. A bit of coral that was found on me—the revolver there which I am supposed to have carried in my pocket. (*To the* SON) Will you not explain where it came from?

SON (*mastering his agitation*): It is my property, sir.

SECOND JUDGE: How did it come into the secretary's possession?

SON: I laid it on the table by my father.

SECOND JUDGE: Valuable information. The revolver, lying on the open table top, prompted the deed. What did you give it to your father for?

SON: I—cannot answer that question.

BILLIONAIRE: I have not betrayed you, either.

SON (*sharply*): Because you know nothing about it.

BILLIONAIRE: You seem to be talking to someone else, not to me. Have I become a stranger to you because I stand under suspicion? (*With a strangely watchful expression*) Do you both believe I am the secretary? You—my own children—are you seeing the secretary in me?

SON (*wearily*): Sir, do you need my sister and me here any longer? (*The* DAUGHTER *screams— covers her face with her hands*.)

SECOND JUDGE: I thank you, no. (*The* SON, *supporting the* DAUGHTER *exit. The* JUDGE *walks up and down the room*.) Monstrous. The utmost extreme of stubborness! Are you not ashamed? (*Disconcerted*) Smiling, are you?

BILLIONAIRE: I saw my children—

SECOND JUDGE: Do you take pleasure in other people's torment?

BILLIONAIRE: But they did not see me.

SECOND JUDGE: They saw the murderer of their father. You are he. You—his secretary. Don't bring your idiotic fairy tale forward again, please—we know it. And were the coral not the powerful proof it is, this would have unmasked you—that those two whom you brazenly pretended were your children, rejected you as an utter stranger.

BILLIONARIE (*imperviously*): That—does not suffice.

SECOND JUDGE: Are you sure? Because you refuse your confession? We excuse you that now. You may continue to shroud yourself in your monumental silence. The time has come for us to speak! (*He signs to the* GUARD *who leads the* BILLIONAIRE *away. The* JUDGE *telephones.*) Relief, please. (*Loudly*) Yes—relief! (*Goes excitedly up and down. Stamps angrily.*) This is . . . (FIRST JUDGE *hastens in, rear.*) You thought you heard wrong, I expect. No, there's no change. The man is not to be caught. He confronts them without a tremor—and finds fault with them for talking coldly to him. (*The* FIRST JUDGE *reads.*) We're done now, I think.

FIRST JUDGE: No. I'm for pressing him hard—this thing interests me. (*Striking his brow*) Simple as daylight!

SECOND JUDGE: Were you enlightened in a dream?

FIRST JUDGE: I am furious.

SECOND JUDGE: Hardly the state of mind for brilliant discoveries.

FIRST JUDGE: He's transsubstantiated himself into the billionaire.

SECOND JUDGE: And expects to stay there.

FIRST JUDGE: Therefore we must now reverse the process—

SECOND JUDGE: Abracadabra—one, two, three.

FIRST JUDGE: And get him back into the secretary.

SECOND JUDGE: By what sleight of hand do you mean to effect this?

(*The* GUARD *comes in at the right and switches off the arc light.*)

FIRST JUDGE: He must be born all over again! That's it! I'll put him back in his cradle and let him kick and crow as happy as the day's long. So far the billionaire has never entered his life—that is a later chapter not to be recalled by a single syllable. I'll set him up such a hole-proof picture of his life and wrap him so gently and gradually in childhood recollections that he shall entirely forget what he's here for. (*Searching through the papers*) We've all the material here—not a detail missing. A strikingly bright and happy past, too; he hasn't hardened all the way through yet. I shall have him as soft as butter once I start bringing his good days back to him.

SECOND JUDGE: He didn't mind facing his victim's children—

FIRST JUDGE: Children are something else. In the last resort it is one's own life that counts.

SECOND JUDGE: I should hate to give up the case as hopeless.

FIRST JUDGE: Everything we've tried so far has fallen through, and my attempt may do the same. But there is a certain power of suggestion in delving into the past.

SECOND JUDGE: Would you like the glasses?

FIRST JUDGE: We'll have the lights down this time. (*To* GUARD) Don't switch on the light. Bring him in. (GUARD *goes, right.*) That alone will be a kindness to him. And for the rest I shall find the right "Now Granny will tell you a story" tone.

SECOND JUDGE: With the wicked wolf at the end.

FIRST JUDGE: That gets hold of the murderer. (*The* SECOND JUDGE *goes. The* GUARD *comes in with the* BILLIONAIRE. *The* FIRST JUDGE *is deep in the documents before him.*) This love of animals is truly beautiful. (*Glancing up at the* BILLIONAIRE) Had it really a black spot in the middle of its forehead? (*The* BILLIONAIRE *raises his head obediently.*) The puppy you saved from drowning. The river was pretty shallow there, I daresay? One doesn't venture very far out at ten years old. (*The* BILLIONAIRE *breathes heavily.*) Just a bit of a stream running by the little town, wasn't it? No strong current, of course—or did the tides run high in spring? (*The* BILLIONAIRE *begins to sway curiously from the waist.*) Then the water would go sweeping by with all sorts of bushes and things it had uprooted, and sometimes it flooded the banks and got into the cellars. That meant saving the family stores, and what a jolly salvaging party it always was! Father and Mother at it as hard as they could go and the boy helping like a Trojan, naturally. Always in everybody's way, but convinced that he was being absolutely indispensable, eh? (*The* BILLIONAIRE *nods slowly*.) Yes—a little bit of a town like that has its catastrophes too. Every day a different one. The wind pulls the cap off a fellow's head and rushes round the corner with it—(*Suddenly*) What color was your school cap—green?

BILLIONAIRE (*with a chuckling smile*): I've ...

FIRST JUDGE: You don't remember the color distinctly?

BILLIONAIRE: I've ... forgotten so much.

FIRST JUDGE (*sharply watching him. After a pause*): Doesn't that sort of thing last long with you? I mean one usually likes to recall one's pleasant times long after they're gone. After all, they're our only indestructible possession. You especially could refresh yourself with your remembrances, for the picture of your past is remarkably charming and bright. Yes, you had an enviable youth. (*Turning over the documents*) It is a pleasure even to read about it. (BILLIONAIRE *stealing a look into the papers*) Light and sunshine—sunshine and light. No trace of a shadow anywhere. (*Glancing up*) You must be inexpressibly grateful to your parents, aren't you?

BILLIONAIRE (*in a tone almost like singing*): My parents. . . .

FIRST JUDGE: I see them with their hands outspread over their only child in a gesture of infinite love. Did they ever once strike you?

BILLIONAIRE: Did they . . . never once strike me?

FIRST JUDGE: Yes, tell me.

BILLIONAIRE: Yes . . . you tell me.

FIRST JUDGE (*looks at him in astonishment. Then jestingly*): Very well, let us now open the Book of the Past. Chapter one—The Home. A little provincial town set in a pleasant green landscape. Father—pastor. Do you see him now?

BILLIONAIRE (*groping before him*): . . . set in a green landscape . . . Father . . . pastor . . .

FIRST JUDGE: Chapter two—The son is born and becomes the center of life at the parsonage. Every care is lavished on him. He waxes and thrives. . . . You will hardly remember your very earliest childhood?

BILLIONAIRE: Now . . . I remember.

FIRST JUDGE: In the next section you're fairly under way. School days. The school is not large . . . there are few pupils, and you are the best among them. Learning comes easily to you . . . you encounter no obstacles . . . this period is a thornless path.

Or perhaps you remember a cloud?

BILLIONAIRE: If you know of none ...

FIRST JUDGE: Good, then there was none. Let's go on. This, then, was the frame in which your life was set. It is seldom that a young man has things made as smooth for him as they were for you ... and your own inclinations met your parents' plans half way. To a rare degree you developed the capacity for becoming a happy man. I can think of nothing finer than this complete harmony between a person and his environment. No disrupting experience to poison the blood ... only the quiet succession of days like flowers on the chains children weave! ... (*Intensely*) Doesn't it flood your heart with warmth to hear me recite this evangel of your past to you? It must awaken in you such wistful longing for that paradise you used to wander in ... in your so cherished and favored youth. Sheltered and loved—protected against the blows that others have to suffer even at that age. It is like looking into a crystal sea, clear down to the very bed where only bright round pebbles lie on the white sand and nothing else. Say yes to that happy past of yours—and save the most precious of all possessions.

BILLIONAIRE: ... the best ... of all possessions. ...

FIRST JUDGE (*in growing excitement*): Do you say yes to that past?

BILLIONAIRE (*faintly breathing the words*): Yes ... yes ... yes! ...

FIRST JUDGE: Now you will sign your deposition.

BILLIONAIRE (*already raising his hand*): Yes.

FIRST JUDGE (*to* GUARD): Undo his hand. (*To the* BILLIONAIRE) Your acquiescence has convicted you. That past is the secretary's. You are the secretary. (As *the* BILLIONAIRE *hesitates*) I am telling you this so that you sign correctly—with the secretary's name. (*The* BILLIONAIRE *writes in the air.*) What are you doing? Can't you remember your own handwriting any more? (*The* BILLIONAIRE *signs.*) The examination is closed. I hope that you will not return again to your former denial of your identity. From now on it would be useless. (*He signs to the* GUARD.)

THE BILLIONAIRE (*as the* GUARD *leads him out, right*): ... The best ... the best ... (*He goes.*)

FIRST JUDGE (*stands thinking. Then telephones*): Comprehensive confession.

SECOND JUDGE (entering): It sounds like a fairy tale really. (*Reads in the dossier.*) Worked like a charm. Didn't he see the trap you were decoying him into?

78

FIRST JUDGE (*ruminating*): Don't you think it extraordinary?

SECOND JUDGE: He was overtired.

FIRST JUDGE: That was not my impression. In fact he seemed to come to life as he listened to his past. (*The* GUARD *enters, right. Quickly*) Has he anything to tell me?

SECOND JUDGE: Hasn't he already gone back to the other?

GUARD: No.

SECOND JUDGE: Has he gone to pieces?

GUARD: He stands up straight, looking upwards and muttering.

FIRST JUDGE: Just as he did here . . . in a dream. . . .

SECOND JUDGE (*after a silence*): Well, there's a terrible awakening in store for him.

ACT FIVE

Small square yard sunk between the shafts of prison walls on four sides. Patch of mean grass with iron bench in the center, fastened into the ground. A low door left and a high, narrow door rear.

GUARD leads BILLIONAIRE in from the left, a convict now in black linen with red neckband.

BILLIONAIRE: The ante-yard of death?

GUARD: You have an hour to stay here.

BILLIONAIRE (*nods*): The last short hour has struck. (*Looking about*) A gentle custom...feet tread upon green grass and heaven's blue streams overhead. (*He stands motionless.*)

GUARD: Do you wish to see your visitors?

BILLIONAIRE: Ah—the curious have come? I shall not resist. (GUARD *goes.* BILLIONAIRE *sits on the bench.* GUARD *admits the* MAN IN GRAY, *and goes.*)

MAN IN GRAY (*has undergone an obvious transformation. His suit—the same color as before—is immaculately tailored. He wears light spats over patent leather shoes; gray top hat with rounded crown, white kid gloves with black stitching. Comes rushing in at the* BILLIONAIRE, *stretching out his hand*): Still in time. This is luck indeed. I should have put in an appearance before this, but business, you know. ... Brimstone mine ... big thing. Yearly profits of ... But for the moment you're rather out of that world of income and dividends and so forth, of course. Besides I didn't come here to talk to you on that subject. I came to thank you.

BILLIONAIRE: I didn't know ...

MAN IN GRAY: You don't mind if I sit down beside you, do you ... on the bench of repentance. One can have at least a quarter of an hour's peace and quiet. Well, then, from the bottom of my heart, thanks, thanks, and thanks again.

BILLIONAIRE: I wish you would tell me.

MAN IN GRAY: I am the Man in Gray who came to you once with a manifest that was to give harmony to all the world at one single stroke—and you refused to sign it. At the same time—the thing I find most admirable about it now is that you should have taken the time; I shouldn't have—you demonstrated to me the hopelessness of my beneficient project. Your arguments struck me like the blows of a club ... and I left the "Warm Heart of the Earth," hurling curses back at you strong enough to fell an ox. Is it getting dark?

Billionaire (*with a thin smile*): You are mistaken.

Man in Gray: I wished you straight into the deepest pit of hell.

Billionaire: Not me. . . .

Man in Gray: You never felt the impact?

Billionaire: Because the conversation you refer to was with the billionaire, not with me.

Man in Gray (*laughs unrestrainedly*): You need not play your role before me. Just put your secretary in your pocket. Or perhaps you haven't one in these pyjamas they put you in for the night without end? (*Tapping him on the shoulder*) You're still my man fleeing from the terror.

Billionaire (*taken aback*): Don't talk so loud.

Man in Gray: Don't worry—I shall neither betray you nor set you free. Surely I have no cause for such an act of ingratitude. Are you satisfied with me?

Billionaire: You are the only one. . . .

Man in Gray: Your trial was a pleasure to me. I wouldn't have disturbed it at any price. It was a stroke of genius to shove yourself into the secretary's skin and lap up the candy of his bright past. I could hear your lips smacking as they kept stuffing you with that glorious grub. How does your stomach feel now—good?

BILLIONAIRE: It was salvation.

MAN IN GRAY: While the son—that rebirth you'd arranged for yourself, all peace and joy, and so forth—turned away from you.

BILLIONAIRE: Not a word of that!

MAN IN GRAY: But you have no more to fear now. And from the safe bank one can look back over the turbulent sea with a malicious joy that is wholesome too. You've saved yourself—and in a few minutes your head won't be in danger from it any more. You can be sure of that.

BILLIONAIRE: What do you thank me for?

MAN IN GRAY: Does not a casual glance upon my outer man tell you that?

BILLIONAIRE: You are dressed with a sort of challenging splendor.

MAN IN GRAY: Merely to illustrate the inner structure. I'm in flight.

BILLIONAIRE: You? From what?

MAN IN GRAY: From the world as you made it.

BILLIONAIRE: Then are you not going to curse me again?

MAN IN GRAY: I bless you. You took me out of my pink clouds and set me on sober earth. Bolt upright on both feet. Your law ruled—flight! Woe to the stumbler, tramp him down. The flight surges over him, on and away. No grace, no mercy. For-ward—forward! ... Chaos is behind!

BILLIONAIRE: And did you gain on it?

MAN IN GRAY: I was a good pupil. I heap up riches and set that glittering hill between them and me. Immense energy develops when once the law is known. Even in sleep one races on and springs out of bed in the morning with new plans ready. A wild chase. Thank heaven you did not take your secret with you to the grave—now I can announce to all mankind its true salvation.

BILLIONAIRE: Will you do that?

MAN IN GRAY: It is already done. My leavings set them all wildly scrambling. All bonds snapped, the fight rages all along the line. Each against each, no hope for quarter.

BILLIONAIRE: And what is the goal you are storm-ing towards?

MAN IN GRAY: Nonsense, there is no goal.

BILLIONARE: But there is.

MAN IN GRAY (*looks at him disconcerted*): Don't torture me.

BILLIONAIRE: It lies in the beginning.

MAN IN GRAY: Yes—you had all the luck. You can afford to laugh at us. Besides you removed the cause that spurs on the race. But that remains a single instance—we can't all find a double in this world. ... And I'll tell you something, too. (*With a gesture round his neck*) And most of us would shy at the price too.

BILLIONAIRE: Do you call it high?

MAN IN GRAY (*standing up*): You can best estimate that yourself according to your own measure. You were never pettifogging when it came to paying the bill. I should like to stay longer, but ... your time is limited too. Anyway let it be some joy to you that your great discovery will not vanish with you. (*Offering both his hands*) Head up, then!

BILLIONAIRE: As long as it lasts.

MAN IN GRAY (*laughs. Waving his hat*): Au revoir!

BILLIONAIRE: Where?

MAN IN GRAY: Well—what is the correct leave-taking in a case like this anyway? (*The* GUARD *opens the door rear. The* MAN IN GRAY *goes. The* BILLIONAIRE *sits on the bench without moving, his chin on the back of his hand. The* GUARD *admits the* SON. GUARD *goes.*)

The SON (*hesitates—then goes quickly to the* BILLIONAIRE, *reaching out his hand*): I have come—to forgive you. (*The* BILLIONAIRE *looks slowly up at him.*) Don't you recognize me?

BILLIONAIRE: Oh, yes.

SON: My decision has taken you by surprise. Perhaps it is strange that a son should do such a thing. But that is the least. I want to save you.

BILLIONAIRE: Have you climbing irons and rope ladder all ready?

SON: I will recognize you as my father. (*The* BILLIONAIRE *stands up and goes behind the bench.*) Don't make it harder for me than it is already. I am as guilty as you, for I had aimed that gun at him, I had meant that very bullet for him, too. It's of no importance who it was that fired.

BILLIONAIRE: This is all incomprehensible to me.

SON: Believe me guilty with you, so that I need not flounder any longer in these frightful things.

BILLIONAIRE: But have you considered what I did?

SON: You did what we must all do at the sight of madness dancing in power.

BILLIONAIRE: Was your father mad?

SON: Power is madness.

BILLIONAIRE: Yes ... he was powerful.

SON: And guilty! Behind your guilt stands his—colossal and inextinguishable. You are his victim as I am—as all others who think at all.

BILLIONAIRE: And do they all desire to kill?

SON: They must—the compulsion is not to be withstood. The temptation comes from those who thrust themselves above them. By force they rise, by force they shall be torn down.

BILLIONAIRE: You make it easy for yourself ...

SON: Did not my final confirmation come from you? I know your life—I read the reports breathlessly as they appeared. The sweetest childhood, the gentlest youth—where was there a sign of impulse to violence?

BILLIONAIRE: Your childhood was no less sweet ...

SON: And yet I sought a weapon when the time came. I meant to punish, being swept away by my sense of justice—you meant to enrich yourself. The sight of force seduced you. My father set you the example—he always acted regardless of others—and so long as such examples are before us, so long will we be tempted.

BILLIONAIRE: Do you mean to wipe out evil example—is that it?

SON: With your help.

BILLIONAIRE: What can I do?

SON: You are to renounce your position so high above the rest of us and come down to our level.

BILLIONAIRE: Your father should do this, you mean.

SON: I shall go to the judge and declare that from this conversation with you I realized that you were my father after all.

BILLIONAIRE: And the coral?

SON: Nothing must stand in the way. We have an immense task before us. The fate of mankind is at stake. We shall unite in the heat of work—and in our untiring zeal we shall be bound together as father and son.

BILLIONAIRE (*shaking his head*): No—I could never so belie myself.

SON: When your life depends on it?

BILLIONAIRE: Because the life you offer me depends on it.

SON: It will take some overcoming. It cost me a struggle to come to you like this. But I did so for the sake of higher things. My father's shadow stands behind you now. Serve this work and you will drive it away.

BILLIONAIRE: Not that way.

SON: I swear to you . . .

BILLIONAIRE: What?

SON: That I will be a son to you—a son who never lost his father.

88

BILLIONAIRE (comes close to him): Shall I name my condition?

SON: Anything.

BILLIONAIRE: Will you be the son to me that your father wished you to be?

SON: What does that mean?

BILLIONAIRE: Go back again to the bank where the sun is shining—then I shall lend myself to your wish. (*The* SON *stares at him.*) Otherwise the shadow that stands behind me will never be driven away.

SON: How are you talking to me?

BILLIONAIRE: Like your father. Is this first test too hard? (*The* SON *looks at him now timidly. The* BILLIONAIRE *puts his hand on his shoulder.*) It is good of you to have come once more. One loves to look at people who are young. Have you not a sister? Was she also ready to accept me as her father? You are decoys, but there are no more bridges. I am only more convinced than ever now. Leave me in my garden here. Green, is it not? And go on to your battlefield. It may be that peace does lead to war, but the man that comes out of that bath of blood tries to save himself. You would not help me, so I took my fate into my own hands. Should you rebuke me now, then, for refusing to lend you my support? (*He leads him toward the left.*) In no hour of your active life are you to abuse me. You have made bold plans ... and if one or other of them should fail ... or if, in the long run, they all should fail ... don't belabor your father's memory with rage and reproaches for his not protecting you against disappointment ... for reasons which it would obviously take too long to go into here. (*The* PRIEST *comes.*) There, you see—the one indispensable element is lacking—time! (*The* SON *goes. The* BILLIONAIRE *stands looking after him. The* PRIEST *has gone to the bench and looks at the* BILLIONAIRE, *turns toward him.*) The third and last guest?

PRIEST: After what I have just seen, my task is very hard. You have received the greatest consolation your fellow men could give you—reconciliation with the son of that unfortunate father.

BILLIONAIRE: You are mistaken. We parted at odds with each other. And if I accompanied him to the door, that was because I was the stronger of the two. I was supporting the defeated.

PRIEST: Did he not come to see you?

BILLIONAIRE: He set a trap for me to fall into. But I was on my guard.

PRIEST: Did he forgive you?

BILLIONAIRE: Had he reason to?

PRIEST: You took his father from him.

Billionaire (*sitting down*): Do you believe in the right of reprisal?

Priest: Earthly things must be allowed to run their course.

Billionaire: I exercised the right of reprisal, nothing more.

Priest: What injury had he done you?

Billionaire: The choice falls blindly ... this one or another. They killed my mother and father both.

Priest (*shrugs his shoulders*): Your parents met a peaceful end.

Billionaire: Then what reason could I have had to kill?

Priest: In an incomprehensible turmoil of spirit you stretched out your hand for another man's riches.

Billionaire (*nods*): In an incomprehensible turmoil—that stamps your wisdom. You roll heaven from over me to breathe in joy beneath. You overwhelm me with your gifts.

Priest (*after a pause*): You wished to have the coral; I have brought it for you. (*The* Billionaire *takes it and looks at it.*) You can dismiss me, if you wish ... or close your ear to my words.

Billionaire: Speak.

Priest (*sits down beside him*): From the refuge

which is opened to us when we leave this life which is like a house with dark windows ...

BILLIONAIRE: Tell me about the house with dark windows.

PRIEST: From that refuge light could enter at a wider door than ...

BILLIONAIRE: Yes, that is it.

PRIEST: And there is no such thing as too late. In one second the infinite treasure may be won.

BILLIONAIRE: What treasure?

PRIEST: The new Being that waits behind this span of life.

BILLIONAIRE: Does it lie in the future?

PRIEST: That future is his who knocks with a humble hand.

BILLIONAIRE (*shaking his head*): The old error remains.

PRIEST: Safe promises are given us.

BILLIONAIRE: Flight into the kingdom of heaven. The cross and vinegar are no salvation. In the end it is not to be found—in the beginning it is there, your paradise.

PRIEST: We are dispossessed ...

BILLIONAIRE: Does that darken recognition? ... I don't want to upset you or knock your tools out of your hand. But the deepest truth will never be proclaimed by you or the thousand of you. It is found always only by one man alone. And it is so enormous that it becomes incapable of all effectiveness. ... You seek a refuge—I could tell you that you are on the wrong path. The goal jumps ahead of you a hundred times over and each time with a blow in your back. And your flight towards sanctuary goes ever more wildly forward. But you never arrive. Not that way ... not that way.

PRIEST: Then tell me this: what is it that gives you—I can find no other word for it—your solemn tranquility?

BILLIONAIRE: I have reached the paradise again that lies behind all of us. A deed of violence brought me through its gates—one needs that, for the angels on either side bear swords of flame. And now I stand amidst the loveliest meadow green. And the blue of heaven streams over my head.

PRIEST: Are you thinking of your pleasant childhood?

BILLIONAIRE: Simple, is it not? "Become like little children ..." Wisdom is only the matter of a phrase, too.

PRIEST: Why can we not remain children always?

BILLIONAIRE: That is a riddle you will not solve today or tomorrow either! (*The* PRIEST *stares out before him.*) ... Do you see this?

PRIEST: It is the coral you asked for as your last request.

BILLIONAIRE: Do you know how it grows out of the bed of the sea? To the surface of the water—no higher. There it stands washed by the tides—moulded by the sea and bound forever to it. Fish are little events that go by in tiny tumult. Fascinating ...

PRIEST: What do you mean?

BILLIONAIRE: Only to open one corner of the case the riddle is enclosed in. What would be best? Never to come out into the storm that drives toward the shore and drags us in its wake. There turmoil roars and drags us into the frenzy of life. We are all driven on ... as we are all driven out of our paradise of quiet. ... Bits broken off the dim coral tree ... wounded from the first day with a wound that does not heal, but burns and burns. It is the fearful pain goads us on our way. ... What is that in your hand? (*He takes the* PRIEST'S *hand with the black crucifix and lifts it high.*) That only dulls the pain. (*He holds the red coral to his breast with both hands.*) This delivers from sorrow! (*The high narrow door is opened. The* BILLIONAIRE *stands up.*)

PRIEST: I cannot go with you.

(*The* BILLIONAIRE *goes towards the door, walking steadily.*)